D0992481

AN
UNCERTAIN
GLORY

Letters of Cautious
but Sound Advice to Stanley,
a Dean-in-Waiting,
from C. F. Coltswood,
a President-at-Large

Frederic W. Ness

AN UNCERTAIN GLORY

Jossey-Bass Inc., Publishers
615 Montgomery Street · San Francisco · 1971

AN UNCERTAIN GLORY
Frederic W. Ness

Jossey-Bass, Inc., Publishers
615 Montgomery Street
San Francisco, California 94111

Library of Congress Catalog Card Number 74-152812

International Standard Book Number ISBN 0-87589-098-9

Manufactured in the United States of America
    Composed and printed by York Composition Company, Inc.
    Bound by Chas. H. Bohn & Co., Inc.

JACKET DESIGN BY WILLI BAUM, SAN FRANCISCO

FIRST EDITION

Code 7120

The Jossey-Bass Series
in Higher Education

General Editors

JOSEPH AXELROD
San Francisco State College
and University of California, Berkeley

MERVIN B. FREEDMAN
San Francisco State College
and Wright Institute, Berkeley

Preface

The life of a college president or dean has always been an interesting one. Even the most casual reader of the current news realizes that the administrator's life these days is more than just interesting. It is exciting, if not downright hazardous. In fact, Mayor John Lindsay not long ago conjectured that the only position in America more difficult than that of mayor of New York City was that of a college or university president.

The task is so preoccupying, in fact, that very few presidents or deans ever have the leisure for reflecting on their calling and still less for sharing their thoughts in writing. When they do write, their active career has usually given way to retirement. Although this fact makes their observations no less valid, it may well give them a slightly different flavor.

The following pages were not written in the heat of battle. But, by a particularly fortunate set of circumstances, they have been produced in what I hope is still my late mid-career. Thanks to a Danforth Foundation short-term administrative leave and the willingness of Chancellor Glenn S. Dumke of the California State Colleges to reassign me temporarily from my duties as president of

Preface

Fresno State College, I was able to devote some time to reflecting on aspects of academic administration which I thought could be of interest both to my fellow practitioners of the art and to those courageous souls who may be contemplating it as a career.

Without their active knowledge I was greatly aided by Robert B. Glenn and Charles E. Glassick, who, serving in my office successively as interns under the program sponsored by the American Council on Education, raised many of the questions to which I have offered answers in this series of imaginary letters.

I am indebted, too, to my colleagues in the Association of American Colleges, Frederick L. Wormald and Elden T. Smith (himself an ex-president), for their many thoughtful suggestions; and to Mrs. Richard D. Weigle, the first lady of St. John's College, for her Letter to Mary, which I have adapted quite without her permission.

And finally I am grateful to my wife, who has shared with me many of the experiences recounted in these pages and, in particular, whose companionship during "our" leave of absence made it possible for me to engage in a lot of long deferred thinking and writing. To her I dedicate this modest effort.

Washington, D.C.   FREDERIC W. NESS
March 1971

Contents

Contents

Contents

AN UNCERTAIN GLORY

Letters of Cautious
but Sound Advice to Stanley,
a Dean-in-Waiting,
from C. F. Coltswood,
a President-at-Large

Prologue

There is, of course, no C. F. Coltswood. Or, at least, no one by that name is now engaged in the rigors of a college presidency. Nevertheless, I have found his fictional existence a great convenience. He provided me with something for which every college dean or president occasionally yearns—a temporary illusion of anonymity. Further, since my own direct administrative experience, while not inconsiderable, is far from comprehensive, his presence made the task of begging, borrowing, and stealing ideas and illustrations far less onerous than it might have been. I hope it may even have provided an illusion of verisimilitude. Finally if anyone were to seek to identify an unnamed administrator who may appear fleetingly in these pages, I can protest at once that he was a friend or associate of Coltswood and not someone known personally to me—not so much an illusion as an escape route.

Such a convenience is not without its price, for I soon found that Coltswood insisted on having his own personality, philosophy, life style, and even a style of expression not necessarily compatible with my own. He would readily admit to being a little old fashioned, even to the extent of being at times a bit fusty. Verbally this ten-

1

dency expresses itself in his preference for polysyllabic words, far-flung metaphors, and a fondness for literary allusions. Such verbal eccentricities are scarcely his worst sins. They are, however, symptomatic of a way of thinking and reacting which may be more reminiscent of the fifties and sixties than of the seventies. I personally can forgive him this pale cast of thought though, for like Coltswood I believe the past does in fact have something to offer the future.

Although Coltswood is of indeterminate age, he inclines to the upper rather than the lower edge of the middle years. He has clearly been around. In the course of his administrative travels he has brushed against, if not locked horns with, a wide range of academic types. He would not claim that, in the process, he has necessarily gained great wisdom. He has, though, acquired some knowledge and expertise, along with at least a modest complement of Machiavellian cunning.

Although he still believes in some of the Puritan virtues, including hard work, his experiences with the changing realities of campus life have clearly had an effect. As a result he would obviously be just as uncomfortable on a reactionary campus as in one of the new experimental colleges. He would intently watch a moon shot, but you would never get him on one of those things. Like many other administrators he is eager to encourage innovation as long as it is not too disruptive. Although he inclines temperamentally toward the status quo, another side of his nature has grown impatient with the sterility of much of contemporary academic tradition.

He is not a philosopher, except in the sense that he is a pragmatist. He is far more interested in the how than the why. In any choice between the thought and the act, he always comes down on the side of the latter. That he may be more concerned with roots and trunks than with branches and leaves in the groves of academe could well be a valid criticism. And yet the philosophers of administration rarely sit in the president's chair.

His young friend Stanley, the recipient of his thoughts on administration, probably got both more and less than he bargained for. His simple request for advice on whether he should aspire to

2

a college deanship or presidency opened the verbal floodgates. Yet from the little we learn about him in the letters we can gather that he is the prototype of a number of courageous younger men and women—may their tribe increase—who are looking toward careers in college or university administration and who may wonder, as they follow the daily news, whether such hazard to life and limb is indeed worth the price. At moments I feared Coltswood's mild disillusionment would turn Stanley off, divert his aspirations into other spheres. But the ultimate essence of the Coltswood spirit is positive and optimistic. Clearly he continues to enjoy himself in college administration. His message to Stanley seems to be to go ahead and give it a try.

What is Coltswood's place in the continuum of higher education? I fear that he may represent the passing of an era. The college presidency or deanship, with all its tribulations, was a gentlemanly, at its best even a scholarly, occupation. Whether it can ever be so again is highly speculative. It could go in the direction of the corporate manager or conversely of the institutional warden. Coltswood and I fully concur, however, in the fervent hope that it will continue to command the services of the educational leader. It is our hope also that these letters will encourage that type of individual to aspire to the uncertain glory of the post.

3

Dear Stanley:

Your letter this morning, as not infrequently happens, brought into focus a half-dozen irrelevancies that have been running in my mind lately. As you can imagine, my leave of absence has opened up the possibility, virtually for the first time since I entered college and university administration thirty years ago, for what Wordsworth termed "powerful feelings recollected in tranquility." I don't pretend that this unfolding has produced any poetry, but it has started considerable reflection about the unpoetic job of the college administrator in these troubled times.

And then, of course, came your letter in which you ask whether I think you should consider a career in college administration after you complete your degree. It may be that you expected a simple yes or no. If so, you asked the wrong person at the wrong time. For as I sit here in Old Heidelberg, the setting where so many brilliant minds over the centuries have pondered the problems of the universe, it would seem almost sacrilegious to answer anything with a simple yes or no—even if one has the ability to do so, which I do not. Moreover, having just read in preparation for this trip James Dundonald's urbane *Letters to a Vice Chancellor,* I am conscious that I may be addressing a future distinguished university administrator and therefore feel a more than ordinary sense of responsibility in replying to your query.

Although a variety of studies in recent years have probed the mysteries of why people go into college teaching, to the best of my knowledge nothing very convincing has come out concerning the why of college administrators. If someone were inclined to such an esoteric investigation, I would urge him rather to investigate why people *stay* in administration.

There is at least one popular fallacy I would dispose of immediately and unequivocally. I refer to the oft-repeated notion that the best administrators are the ones who least desire to administer. I have even known deans and one or two presidents to protest that they were shanghaied out of the classroom, to which they would return the instant they could persuade the trustees to unshackle the bonds. Nonsense!

The successful presidents and deans I have known were in administration because they wanted to be in it and stayed because they had some sort of masochistic love for it. What this says about their character is probably not an appropriate theme for a letter. On the other hand, I believe their success lies partially in the fact that they have adopted a kind of humanistic approach, seeing administration as a scholarly discipline with an inherent integrity and value.

I am candid enough to admit also that most of us are in this business because we instinctively like to be in positions of authority. We do not even pale at being called the Establishment. I would not have you believe for a moment, though, that this distinguishes officers of administration from officers of instruction, to use terms that were current back in the thirties and forties and that deserve to be revived. I have known as many teachers who are in the classroom because they like a feeling of power, of displaying their vastly superior knowledge before a vastly inferior audience, as I have deans or presidents who respond to comparably base motives. I would even suggest that the man who does not relish the power that accompanies such responsibilities will be very uncomfortable in the exercise of administrative authority. There undoubtedly is a place for him, but it is not in the office of the dean or of the president.

Which brings me to some additional speculation as to why certain academic administrators succeed where others fail. In a few instances the answers are all too easy to find. I think of my friend Leonatus, who was ambitious, talented, articulate, charming, attached to a wealthy wife, and thus seemingly had all the attributes for instant success as a college president. Unfortunately, he combined an affection for vintage wines with an inability to handle the deleterious side effects. On the other hand, one of the great university presidents whom I have known more than casually could start off the evening by out-vodkaing a cossack, dance a dozen Polish polkas at midnight, and talk German philosophy until dawn. I do not, I hasten to add, advance this talent as prerequisite to successful administration, particularly if you aspire toward the church-related college; but, in reverse, the tragicomedy of my friend Leonatus was that he soon found his bibulous proclivities incompatible with administration. In scholarly fairness I must conclude that both these examples are fairly untypical. You will find, I'm sure, that we presidents are on the whole a fairly sober lot—even when away from campus.

Another rather common reason for failure lies at either extreme of sensitivity. Believe me, for a top college officionado it is as bad to be insensitive as it is to be hypersensitive. As incredible as it may seem, these two weaknesses can be combined in one person. A president of my acquaintance was at one and the same time hyperconsiderate of his own ego and hypercallous to the needs and interests of others. Moreover, he was also blessed with an inordinate ambition and an easy virtue. This man, who before he became president was seen more than once with tears running down his cheeks because of some real or fancied slight from his predecessor, became a veritable lion when he himself succeeded to office. He clearly believed in doing unto others what had been done unto him, and ironically it took nearly a decade for him to get his comeuppance. You may well ask how such a person could ever have become a university president, but that too is another story. Ultimately both students and faculty rose in adequate dudgeon, and the trustees accepted his resignation with minimal regret. How many years will be required for the institution to heal its wounds would be hard to say.

I am not suggesting, Stanley, that a certain amount of self-esteem is not essential. Without it I doubt that any of us could long sustain the abuse which is part of the administrator's lot. Unfortunately, the occupation seems to induce a state closer to overweening egotism than to self-esteem. Presidents, even deans, customarily receive V.I.P. treatment (even the militants reserve special treatment for them); people do defer to them or seem to do so. After a certain amount of this, some of them come to believe that they are in truth figures of some stature. They then tend to lose perspective and, what may be more important, the ability to laugh at themselves. They expect to take their place at the head of the line and visibly resent being asked for tickets at athletic and cultural events. Lese majesty!

One of the essential qualities of a successful college dean or president is an interest in and empathy for other people, including students and faculty. I think of an episode out of my own administrative past when I was serving under the most efficient, even brilliant, man whom I have ever known. I could extol his virtues at inordinate length. But he had one besetting vice which led ultimately, not exactly to his downfall, but at least to the frustration of his ambitions. He simply had minimal interest in people as such. The time came in his career when he would have been the logical choice to succeed to the college presidency; but in the political scramble which inevitably accompanies such transitions, no one came forward to support his candidacy and he finished in the hinterlands.

Another reason for the failure of college administrators was articulated back in the last century by Thomas Arnold of Rugby fame when he cautioned, "No one should meddle with the university who does not understand it and love it." Unfortunately, the woods are full of meddlers who somehow or other get into administrative positions. Whether there could ever have been such a person here at Heidelberg is conjectural; since the rector is normally in office for one year only (though I believe this is being changed), he presumably could do little damage anyway. On the other hand the tradition in the United States has all too often encouraged trustees to give long-term presidential appointments to retired generals and admirals, prospective bishops, exhausted business executives, and the like, men with no presumptive affection for academic administration. Although some of these have been brilliant successes, others have been so unfamiliar with and even unsympathetic toward academia that their administrations have had disastrous consequences.

But, Stanley, after all of these comments, comments that suggest either the "Happy Warrior" or "tragic flaw" rationale for administrative success or failure, I have a terrible revelation to

7

make. Presidential success or failure is, I fear, largely a matter of luck. I vaguely recall some story, possibly of Mark Twain's, about a man who would have been the greatest general ever known if the recruiting office had allowed him to enlist, if there had been a war, and if he had been in it. The analogy is far from exact, of course. The college president is almost always in a war, and whether he wins or loses bears only a marginal relation to his foresight, his knowledge, his wisdom, his charm, his blood pressure, his . . . and I could go on. Although old Gloucester in *King Lear* said very little else that was particularly perceptive, his remark about the stars above governing our condition certainly applies to college presidents. I am sure, if you don't insist on breaking off this correspondence, that I shall offer some further comment on this happy theme.

Before I close, though, let me declare that I clearly belong to the Dodds-of-Princeton school of thought, which holds that academic leadership belongs to academicians. Not that we are born under more favorable stars but only that our background renders us generally better able to play the odds in this particular game of chance. So go on for your doctorate and with your getting you will acquire either enough knowledge to avoid some of the administrative flaws I have just talked about or perhaps even enough wisdom to stay out of college administration altogether.

I am sure you will not assume that these are the only causes of failure or that I have known only administrators who failed. Perhaps in a subsequent letter—remember, you raised the question—I can cover a few of the other pluses and minuses to successful administration. Meanwhile, it is time to pack our bags and drive further south. As we pass through this lovely country where your ancestors and mine, some two hundred and twenty-five years ago, set out for the heartland of Pennsylvania, I wonder why they left.

Cordially,
Charles

Dear Stanley:

From the balcony of our hotel room we can see Mt. Pilatus in the distance. According to legend, Pontius Pilate was transplanted here with the clear anticipation that the snowy peak would prove inimical to his Mediterranean blood.

He was, you will remember, a man who had some difficulty making up his mind. You will forgive me, I hope, if I use this as the theme for my second brief letter on some of the perils of university administration. For the test of an administrator lies basically in the quality and timing of his decisions. Perhaps I should also have included "quantity" as an important characteristic, but I am not so sure.

Some years ago I was asked to speak to a group of hospital administrators on the art of decision making, which was the first time I ever gave it much conscious thought. I discovered, somewhat to my surprise, that the subject was highly involved and that a number of unreadable books had been devoted to it, mostly for the enlightenment of industrial management. I would not have you expect anything more in this letter, however, than a kind of genial approach to the topic. With your scholarly proclivities, I have little doubt that you will know where to turn if you wish to pursue it in more detail.

There was the old-time administrator—in fact, I succeeded one in a college presidency—who reportedly allowed no one to make any independent decisions. Inevitably this kind of man involves himself in an enormous number of problems which should have been handled by other members of his staff. While today's administrative salaries are still far from what they should be for executives of comparable ability and responsibility, annual compensation of $18,000 or above is not at all uncommon for second, third, or even fourth echelon administrators. Anyone in that salary bracket, I would maintain, can be expected to accept the responsibility of making decisions, even the big ones. If he cannot, he should be transported to some snow-clad peak of his own. If he can and is not permitted to, his frustration will soon encourage him to migrate.

This is not to say that the president is to be removed from the decisional level when it is a matter affecting the well-being of the college. He obviously must be kept informed and the sooner the better. But one of the worst things that can happen is for him to be brought into the decision-making process prematurely. This error narrows too quickly his area of maneuverability. He should remember that he is also something of a teacher: he has a responsibility to assist his staff in its own learning process. I have, accordingly, over the years developed the technique of always asking any member of my administration who brings a problem to me how he proposes to resolve it. (You will notice that I said "resolve" rather than "solve." As an old dean whom I knew used to observe: "Most of our problems have no solutions; the best we can do is seek some resolution, and then pray earnestly for absolution.")

I would observe—though this is not likely to strike you with amazement—that a vast majority of the decisions which a dean or president has to make are decisions relating to people. Whereas our new offices of institutional research provide us with data in mounting volume, these are useful normally only for those relatively few major policy decisions which we have to make from time to time. Even then, they often involve outcomes which are almost childishly obvious when the facts are laid on the table. For example, a careful cost analysis department by department makes relatively easy the determination of where to allocate resources. Similarly, studies of enrollment trends are so patently vital to good long-range planning that only the least sophisticated institutions have not built such studies into their administrative routine.

It is the "human" decisions that have to be made, usually

with a minimum of information, which cause gray hair and sleepless nights. Should a certain troublesome instructor be reappointed in the hope that he will grow up, or will this simply prolong the inevitable and make it all the more traumatic? Would it be better to require this particularly immature student to withdraw in the hope that military service might aid the maturation process? On the other hand, if he were killed or maimed, would I feel a sense of personal responsibility? Is the English department recommending the appointment of Assistant Professor X because he is qualified to teach or because he has been fired from College Y in the heat of controversy?

It is too bad, I guess, that we can't see into the minds of our fellow naked apes. Probably what we would see would be too frightening. But some can do it. I remember asking a wily old administrator, when I was still young in this business, to provide me with some insights into one of the deans about whom I had growing misgivings. "Oh, Dean X," he said, "he is a very remarkable man. I have never known anyone who could more quickly discover what makes another person tick. His only trouble is that he doesn't know what to do about it then!"

There is little doubt that the character of an administrator can be seen in the style of his decisions. I think of one man who became a vice-president at a remarkably early age, after notable success in industrial management. I should add that he had all the necessary credentials, including an Ivy League doctorate. According to his associates, however, he was one of those men who felt that failure to make instant decisions on every issue brought to his attention would be interpreted as youthful weakness. Even though his batting average was fairly good—twenty-five per cent on the right side is considered to be the national average—his peculiar staccato style seemed to create a lack of respect on the part of his associates. The story has a happy ending, however, for he subsequently moved on to head a large university and, at least from my distant prospect, I should say that he was quite successful. Possibly the job became so demanding as to persuade him to be a little more relaxed in his decision-making style; or perhaps the tempo of decision making de-

11

manded by his new job just suited his personality and temperament.

One of the most remarkable college presidents whom I ever knew—and I knew him approximately twenty-five years before he assumed the headship of the university which he had served in various other capacities during all that period—never said "no" to anybody under any circumstances. Equally, he never quite said "yes." And he managed to get away with it! He was surely the most successful buck passer in academic history, but he did it with such geniality that only the most irascible could take offense. I think of him even today with the warmest affection, but thank heaven I no longer have to work with him. He was quite the reverse of the financial officer in the same university who kept a sign on his desk which read, "Before you ask, the answer is no." But with such a president maybe this type of undergirding was not inappropriate.

President X was a firm decision maker. He ran what was often referred to as a taut ship—appropriate enough since he had once served in the navy. It was so taut, in fact, that eight or so years before Berkeley changed the complexion of campus life in America, he discharged four students for daring to take a drink off campus and campus reaction was stormy. Through the efforts of several of his more moderate aides, calm was restored and for several months he himself seemed almost to exercise a gentling influence. With the opening of school in the fall, however, his true nature reemerged, and in a public statement he declared that the difficulties of the previous spring had occurred because the students had not been subjected to sufficiently rigid discipline. The next disruption did not occur for several years, possibly because the hatches were secured so tightly. When it did occur, however, in the early sixties, it was of such violence that the campus had to be swept by the state police, a number of arrests were made, and the president was forced to resign.

I have just made a decision, which is to bring this discussion to a close. It needs, though, a few added admonishments. First, some decision makers are born that way, and many of their associates wish they never had been. The rest of us, I suspect, have had to learn the hard way. In this process I have discovered several things I have never read in any of the books.

The first is that you should never make a decision until you have to, or better phrased, you should never make a decision prematurely. For very often a problem will resolve itself and do so in a way much better than might have been accomplished by any deliberative action. But I must add a word of caution. Delay can easily be interpreted as indecision, with the result that other members of the ship's crew can get terribly uneasy. In the thick of the storm this can be disastrous.

Second, don't feel that you have to do *something* about *everything*. In my early years as a dean, it seemed that everybody who entered the sacred portals of my office began with, "Sir, I have a problem." Although I don't remember ever actually doing it, I many times felt like replying, "Who in the . . . doesn't?" Even when the complaints may be thoroughly legitimate and even when they almost literally tear at your heartstrings, don't always try to do anything about them. Often it is enough merely to give the other person a chance to get it off his chest. Remember, Christ lived on this earth some thirty-three years, at a time when the injustices of the world were certainly no fewer than in our own era. But He elected to fight only certain battles. To have taken on them all would probably have rendered Him largely ineffectual. (Of course, He might have lived longer had He tackled the easier ones at the expense of the more difficult.)

But always hear them out. For what most people want is someone to listen to them. Years ago, while I was still a dean, I told one of my children that I planned to retire from the rigors of a deanship and hang out a shingle reading "Charles F. Coltswood, Ph.D., Listener." My normal fee would be $25 per session. If sympathy were required the fee would be $30. On my next birthday, when I unwrapped his present, there was my shingle beautifully done up in mahogany. With it was another and smaller one to be attached with either side out as appropriate. One side bore the words "Receptive Today," and the other added the word "Not." But the dean and president must really always keep the positive side showing.

Third, listen all you wish to, but never make a decision over

13

the head of the person who really should be making it. This is so obvious that I almost apologize for mentioning it. But unfortunately I have seen it happen, even in a more invidious form in which the top man makes a decision on the advice of the appropriate sub-altern on his staff and then, when confronted with it, says in effect, "Well, I followed the advice of the dean, why don't you take this up with him." Need I say more? The young instructor in one such instance during my deanship hasn't spoken to me to this day. Neither of us is any longer very young.

Fourth—and forgive me, Stanley, I hadn't intended this to go on and on—touch all bases. No college president has time to do anything thoroughly. This is an occupational hazard. But, and I offer this as Coltswood's First Law, it takes less time to touch bases than to mend fences. To me, this is the main justification for delaying decisions, beyond the usually futile hope that the problem will dry up and go away.

Fifth, don't overlook the ineluctability of battle fatigue. I have observed administrative teams whose combined IQs would reach astronomical totals but who, under prolonged stress, can absolutely not avoid making a disastrous decision. For this I have no advice. The American college campus, as I sit here so many thousands of miles away, is the main focus of a social revolution. Very few administrators, by either temperament or training, are cut out for this sort of thing. And that is perhaps why, despite the ultimate message of *King Lear,* I suspect that old Gloucester may have been right: our fates are indeed determined by the "stars above."

Sixth, don't underestimate the trivial decision, for it can have a more catastrophic effect than many a presumably major decision. For example, it would seem almost immaterial whether a new president should decide to have an inaugural ceremony or be satisfied with a simple installation. The difference, however, can well run into the tens of thousands of dollars. A decision to send a vice-president to the railroad station to meet an eccentric donor and his wife rather than go himself once cost a university president a new art center. If your college doesn't have a mace or a presidential seal when you take office, wait a year or two before deciding to add them to the panache of your official regalia. Also, if you decide your office needs refurbishment, since your predecessor's taste was that of another century, you will do well to avoid haste and extravagance. Otherwise you may find you have created an extravagance for your successor to enjoy, and that rather prematurely.

And finally, strange as it may seem, I have discovered that decisions are easier when you are in a position where you cannot pass the buck. This observation, I know, appears to make little sense; but I am convinced that there is a world of difference between being the number two man and the number one man in the ease with which an administrator can accept and execute the responsibilities of his office. So long as he knows that someone immediately above him can reverse him and in any case will have to take the final responsibility, it is all the more difficult for him to make firm and positive decisions. For this reason the second man often appears to the other denizens in the jungle to be just a bit watery in the knees (if I may scramble my metaphors). But make him king of the jungle, and he will pour milk with the best of them.

And although I know I have already said "finally," this time I mean it—finally, except in the most incredibly serious situation, never rebuke a subordinate for exceeding his authority. Rebuke him only (and this most gently) for not exercising his authority.

Yr. Faithful Servant,

Charles

Dear Stanley:

Strange recollections sometimes occur when one is on a middle-aged holiday. Yesterday as the train bearing our car disappeared into the long darkness of the St. Gotthard Tunnel, I recalled that lovely passage from an old Anglo-Saxon chronicle wherein the poet was describing life as the flight of a bird entering from the darkness into the firelit mead hall, winging through the warmly glowing interior, and passing out the other end again into the darkness. Our half-hour hegira, of course, had the situation in reverse, which may be an appropriate way of thinking negatively about the possibility of your going into university administration. Rather than considering what you might gain or contribute by becoming a dean or president, I want to spend just a moment or two in this early morning hour, as I look out over Lake Lugano in the misty sunlight, thinking of some of the things that you will have to give up.

Knowing you as I do, I can predict that one of the most difficult things you will have to give up will be the opportunity to continue as a scholar in your own discipline. In fact this may well be the deciding factor in your situation. You can try the mix, and I know you would try, but administration is simply a full-time job and slightly more. It has another peculiarity, too, which militates against scholarship, and that is its circus-like aspect which makes impossible the administrator's sticking with any one project more than a few moments of the time. Scholarship's requirement of long hours of concentration is habit forming. So is the administrator's kaleidoscopic regimen. Except in the rara avis, the two simply do not conjoin.

16

You may remember, though, my first letter, in which I postulated that a successful administrator is one who is able to transfer a scholarly interest from his academic discipline to his new calling in administration. And here, I suggest, is a saving grace. You did, after all, make a gradual transition into your present level of interest in literary scholarship. Is there any reason, therefore, why you could not make still another transition? There are even certain rewards in this, for an almost voracious tribe of editors is looking for literate articles and books on administrative subjects. To be sure, the articles they publish rarely provide for footnotes and an expatriot scholar at first feels rather naked; but I can assure you that this too shall pass. In fact, it is passing as new, energetic scholars are turning their attention to the problems of administration. But few of them are at the same time practicing administration.

Another joy which one must generally forego when he drops the scholar's mantle for the administrator's mace is the joy of teaching. You have as yet only limited experience as an instructor, and I am uncertain how dedicated you are to the art. I would have to say, in candor, that it was not terribly difficult for me to make the transition, largely because I had intended to go into administration even before I entered graduate school. Nevertheless I still feel a kind of conventional envy of those of my administrative colleagues who return permanently to the classroom. It is not impossible, of course, that they had left it prematurely in the first place.

Recently, one of our faculty committees, in designing (as faculty committees are fond of doing) an elaborate set of guidelines for administrators, suggested that every one under the level of president be required to teach at least one course per semester. This virtuous requirement would have my full support except for one participant—the student. The conscientious administrator is also a conscientious teacher, and except under the rarest of circumstances, where his discipline is directly related to his administrative responsibilities or where his genius provides for a happy schizophrenia, he will discover as I did that to leap blithely from confronting an administrative contretemps to the delivery of a lecture on Shakespeare's fools requires a psychological transition beyond the capacity

17

of most of us. (I have said nothing, of course, about the difficulty of keeping up with one's discipline and of preparing for the hour in the classroom while one is locked on the administrative treadmill, but this would seem almost too obvious.)

You may feel at first blush that neither of these sacrifices is too great. If so—and please do not think I am trying to discourage you—let me try a few others. In view of my exquisite location at the moment—sitting on a balcony looking at the sarcenet mists across Lake Lugano—it may sound hypocritical for me to point out that one of the things an administrator gives up is the possibility of a sabbatical. The Danforth Foundation, convinced that this is too great a sacrifice, recently initiated a program to try to convince boards of trustees that presidents and deans need to get away fully as much as do faculty members. In fact, the possibility exists that a campus is better off if they do disappear periodically! But this is quite literally the first time in nearly thirty years that I have had more than thirty consecutive days away from the job; whereas many of my faculty colleagues are confirmed sabbatical-goers. I would add, with a touch of pique, that quantitatively my list of publications is quite up to most of theirs!

Then there are those regular vacations within the year—Thanksgiving, Christmas, spring vacation, Indian summer, Guy Fawkes Day, and the like—which, though always available to faculty members, are for the most part denied the shopkeepers in the deans' and presidents' offices. And in the same vein, although the conscientious instructor certainly puts in at least a fifty-five hour week, there is nevertheless a subtle but real time clock psychology which dominates his administrative colleagues. We are not exactly manacled to the desk, but if we were to turn around fast enough we would see the bitter end of that long chain around the corner as we leave the office.

In the proper spirit of saving the worst to the last, let me caution you that one of the things you may well have to give up if you succumb to the blandishments of top administration is friendship—friendship, that is, with members of the faculty and even with other members of the administration. I realize that this is as

18

debatable as many of the other ideas I have been bandying, but if you plan to spend your life in one of those small or medium-sized colleges that still preserve the fiction of being an "academic community," both you and Mary will never be quite sure, no matter where you go in a social situation with members of the faculty, that you are really part of the "old gang." From Mary's standpoint, she may well wonder if people are being nice to her because they like her or because they think they can wheedle some information out of her. From your standpoint, if you become too friendly with any particular members of the faculty you will find yourself shortly being accused of "administration by crony" or at the very least of playing favorites in making those tough final decisions about promotion, tenure, and so forth. The fact that many of these decisions are now virtually mandated by faculty peer groups will not immunize you from such criticism. Academic fictions linger long after academic facts—to be known hereafter as Coltswood's Second Law.

And for this, Stanley, you can expect at the age of fifty to make roughly the same salary for twelve months that you would have made had you stayed in the classroom on a nine-month contract.

Ruefully,
Charles

Dear Stanley:

As academic disquisitions these letters may smack a bit of the travelogue. They probably share the shortcomings of both. Today in Verona we did the proper thing and visited the supposed domicile of Juliet, and I did the proper thing by taking my Juliet's picture under the balcony. Ah, Romeo. . . .

It is a little hard to believe that so charming a city could have housed so tragic a debacle. Shakespeare saw it, among other things, as a battle between youth and age—which has a peculiarly contemporary ring. I may want to comment on this conflict in another letter, but our visit here in Verona set up another train of thought which I would like to pursue. I am thinking particularly of the contrasts between what one might expect from so fair a setting as an ancient city or an ancient university and what one all too often finds.

I have had a number of friends and colleagues over the years who entered the academic world after a lifetime in business or industry (I suppose there is still a difference between the two). They did so in a spirit of wide-eyed expectation. After the ceaseless strife of money-grubbing competition, they approach the campus much like the poet in "Ode on a Distant Prospect of Eton College." Now, I would not want you at your early age to become cynical. Far better that you should find some of these things out for yourself gradually. On the other hand, the academic world is a jungle, and whereas the administrator plays a variety of hairy roles, he is rarely either Tarzan *or* the King of the Beasts. He is merely a well-meaning denizen trying to earn an honest dollar.

20

I learned this rather bitter lesson when, shortly after entering college administration in the lowly role of "assistant to ————," the president of the institution was forced into retirement. It is hard for me to believe, even at this remove, some of the creatures that came out from behind the woodwork. Had the academic and financial vice-presidents combined forces or, with or without them, had the deans of the component schools got together, they could very well have resisted the Machiavellian power play by several of the trustees. But nobody worked with or scarcely even talked to anybody else. Each had his own horse to back. The result was more than a year of the most appalling infighting bordering ever on imminent chaos. The Board ultimately appointed one of its own members to the presidency. At this point the faculty, which had previously been quiescent, rose to a man and demanded his resignation, a demand to which he angrily yielded. An acting president of questionable stature was put in office and served mundanely for nearly two years before a permanent appointment became possible.

A well-known tradition calls for implacable enmity between faculty and administration. So many words have been written on this by so many wise owls that I don't care to add my hoot. What is less often recognized—at least I have not seen it in writing—is that the principle of territoriality is continuously at work even within the administrative cadre. For example, I have rarely known an academic vice-president and a financial vice-president to work together long without quasi-volcanic eruptions. My first suspicion of this was when, as a young man, I found that the real censor of the president's annual report, which it was my job to ghostwrite under the aegis of the academic vice-president, was not the president or academic vice-president but the financial vice-president. I do not suggest that his criticisms were invalid. Anything delivered with such vigor must have validity! But I do recall that his observations were by no means limited to the fiscal sections of the report.

When I moved next into a line position at another institution I discovered that my counterpart on the financial side customarily flowed like water into any low or unprotected area. He had, in fact, been making what I considered essentially academic decisions for years; and changing this tradition was, I assure you, a ceaseless and bloody struggle. On one occasion I discovered that, in his role as ultimate comptroller of the bookstore, he had refused to order copies of a Henry Miller novel asked for by one of the more controversial instructors. Regardless of the literary or even moral merits of the case, I could not brook such interference. Within minutes I had stormed into the president's office and demanded that he order the financial vice-president to appear and then that he make a decision as to which of us was responsible for the academic management of the campus. Although I usually won, such is the life of scholarship in the jungles of academia!

After running into this conflict in two subsequent administrative assignments I nearly concluded that it was a function of my own personality—probably the projection of an otherwise unsinister Oedipus complex or merely the residual of an early sibling rivalry. Then one day I happened to mention the subject to an old friend who had spent many years in collegiate administration. In our discussion of the proper role of the financial officer in policy formulation we discovered that, from our different but somewhat parallel experiences, we had both seen an almost unavoidable tendency for the fiscal tail to wag the academic dog. He told me, for example, that in one of the western states there was a kind of witticism in which it was claimed that the three greatest educators in the country were James Bryant Conant, Logan Wilson, and whoever was the current director of finance in the state. Oddly enough, the financial officer tends to base judgments not on whether the cost of the project is reasonable but on whether the project itself is valid. Thus I suspect that the reasons for this natural conflict have to do far less with the type of personality attracted to the respective positions than with an overlap of interests and an unclear delineation of responsibilities. Quite obviously the chief business of an academic institution is academic business. Inevitably, therefore, the financial officer, whose responsibility is budget control, will have an instinctive yen to make academic judgments. The dean or academic vice-president, if he is worth his salt, must fight this every inch of the way.

I have experienced a situation in which the chief financial

officer of the college was also the treasurer of the board of trustees, with the result that even the president had his authority challenged by this character from time to time in a manner scarcely to be tolerated. This was resolved only when the number-one candidate for successor to the president refused to accept the offer until the situation was corrected. In the meantime, though, he was the second highest paid man in the institution and, it follows, nearly the first in power. Since I came up the academic ladder I obviously believe that the academic dean or vice-president must be second only to the president, unless there is an executive vice-president who serves as the president's alter ego. Even in this case, though, the chief academic officer must report directly to the president and not through an intermediary.

But this raises the whole panoply of fascinating questions about the organization and pecking order of the central administration, which is far more than I can deal with this morning. I am sure it can wait for another day. Meanwhile, my continental breakfast is long since finished, and since we have many miles to cover and dates to keep, I shall close with another useful observation on academic administration, an observation which one ignores at his own peril: "Everything in academic life is vastly more charged with emotion than with intellect."

Yours fondly,

C. J.

Dear Stanley:

So far as I am concerned Venice is an immortal love affair. Yesterday on the Grand Canal we saw where Browning and Donizetti, Verdi and Wagner played out some of their passions. We were also shown by our illiterate encyclopedia of a gondolier named Armando where Desdemona allegedly lived and was courted by Othello. If so, this is the same house where "honest" Iago accompanied his lord during the courting.

Which brings me to a question that I think deserves at least some brief consideration—the question of administrative honesty. The traditional concept of the president is that he is some kind of Machiavellian scoundrel. You have probably heard of the apocryphal meeting between two almost legendary presidents, the young Charles Eliot of Harvard and the more seasoned Nicholas Murray Butler of Columbia (whom I met in his later years). Eliot was deeply concerned because one of his faculty members had just called him a liar. Butler hastened to comfort him: "Oh, don't let that worry you, Charles, I have frequently been called a liar. What's more, the faculty has more than once been able to prove it."

I was rather dramatically reminded of this story a few days before departure when one of the young campus militants came into my office, looked me intently in the eye, and asked, "Do you think you are honest?" Not being a Nicholas Murray, the only thing I could do was answer him honestly and say yes. But the very fact that I am taking your time to talk on this theme implies that the subject is a rather uneasy one.

I have known well, for approximately twenty-five years, a

24

former college president who is unquestionably a man of great personal integrity—in most things. He had a distinguished career, and in many ways he was an extremely effective administrator. If he wanted something badly enough, however, he seemed to feel that the ends justified the means. In discussing employment with prospective candidates, for example, he made promises he could not fulfill. The results for many a hapless individual were frustration and at times even heartache. On one occasion he promised a young economist a substantial beginning salary plus increments far beyond those available to anyone else on the staff. Even more incredible, he promised a new member of the administration extra salary for running the evening school when in fact there was no evening school and hadn't been for several years.

Generally speaking, a medical doctor is fortunate in that his patients cannot, in any large numbers, get together to discuss his skill. A college dean or president, on the other hand, bears no small resemblance to the warden of an institution. He is inevitably the subject of a great deal of discussion, speculation, and interchange of intelligence. Further, as I observed in an earlier letter, he is generally leaping from one subject to another every few minutes. Thus, unless he has a phenomenal memory or a constantly recording pen, it is inescapable that he will be found guilty from time to time of certain inconsistencies. When this has happened on a sufficient number of occasions and when there has been the usual exchange of intelligence among his students or faculty colleagues, he is a fortunate man indeed if he can maintain unsullied his reputation for integrity.

The subject has another dimension as well. The president is the focus of an infinite variety of conflicting interests which, like a juggler, he must somehow keep in proper rhythmic sequence. It would be too much to expect, therefore, that his answers would always be unequivocal as he tries to say "no" so as not to offend or, more likely, so as to retain a degree of loyalty from students, faculty, or staff which might some day be useful. And here again, there is a limit to the number of evasive answers an administrator can give without jeopardizing the integrity of his position.

As I reread this last paragraph I think I have perhaps been somewhat infelicitous. For the problem is not really one of being evasive. Evasiveness and equivocation are as difficult to get away with as a "no comment" in a press conference. The ideal is, of course, to state truthfully as much as it seems possible and/or prudent to say at the moment. This principle may produce answers like "I haven't made up my mind," "I just can't tell you now," "I will do the best I can for you," "I'm sympathetic to your proposal but can't make a definite commitment right now"—but they are not equivocal or evasive. They may well get you the reputation of being a canny bird, but over the long pull they will tend to create confidence that you don't fudge or make hollow promises. The ultimate aim of all this is to avoid any appearance of manipulating people in breach of the Kantian imperative.

From all this, Stanley, I would offer only one piece of fatherly advice. Don't give a second thought to the reputation you may have for honesty or lack thereof. It is true that you have to live with your colleagues. But it is much more relevant that you have to live with yourself. Set your own standards of integrity— and I am sure you will set them high—and compromise them only in extremis.

And from this high level of philosophical abstraction, since Marjorie has not as yet finished packing her bags, let me descend to a very practical question nearly every top administrator has to face—the question of "cumshaw." I refer to those innocent little gifts, Christmas or otherwise, that come from grateful concessionaires, worried parents, even an occasional student whose intentions, of course, are always of the purest. This giving of gifts is, I grant you, as old as the ancient Greeks, which, as they themselves observed, makes it nonetheless suspect. The problem, though, is often what to do about it. In one instance, many long years ago, I learned of some gifts from a supplier to one of our university officials which seemed to me a little excessive. These included not only some living room furniture and a turkey at Christmas but a color TV as well. After an uneasy night I decided to discuss the problem with the president. Whereupon the good gentleman confessed to me that he had received and accepted the same gifts that had been bestowed upon his subordinate!

Having just read Pearson and Anderson's *The Case Against Congress,* I must recognize that the giving of gifts is not just an old Greek custom but an American one as well. I have always maintained a rigid policy, however, of refusing to accept presents for my own use except from personal friends; and, amazingly enough, have still managed to keep my wife and children clothed and fed. The problem is that this policy is not without a price. What do you do, for example, when the gift is perishable as, say, a crate of oranges? Well, there is always a nearby hospital which, if the perishable is also edible, is usually cooperative. The thank-you note to the donor should, of course, be precisely informative. On one occasion when to return the gift would have been quite ungracious I handed it over to my secretary with the explanation, "Just because I refuse to accept bribes should not prevent your doing so." In that instance I quid-pro-quo'd by dispatching to the donor an autographed copy of one of my recent books. In another instance my thank-you note specified that the gift, a silver bowl, would be used only for official college entertaining—and it was. Only once did I go to the not inconsiderable personal expense of mailing a gift back to the donor. What's more, his son was *not* readmitted!

The truth is, the college president, if he is so inclined, has lots of little ways to benefit from his position. Often it is much more trouble to avoid than to decline. I heard of one president, for example, who never paid when he went past the cashier in the cafeteria. Not only did my informant know of it, but so did everyone else on campus. And it was generously remembered when he was ultimately forced to resign for some less innocuous indiscretions, including an all-expense-paid trip to the Orient. Ironically, the man could well have afforded to pay for himself, for he had substantial income from outside business interests.

I have never, on the other hand, hesitated to accept honoraria for speeches or consultation fees, particularly where these involve, as invariably they do, effort over and above the call of duty. "Booster" speeches in behalf of the college, talks to educational or

27

church groups (when I cannot get out of them) are excepted. But all too often we allow ourselves to be abused by those who are merely looking for inexpensive or free entertainment, and I do not consider roast beef and peas adequate compensation. Whether you then should wish to turn your pittance over to your favorite charity is a matter of conscience; but I do so only after I can think of no way to use it for private recreation—and in this area I seem to have a most fertile imagination.

And now, my friend, I see my Desdemona is packed. The time has come to leave this storied dream of Venice and push on to the south. Andiamo! y

a rivederci

C. J.

Dear Stanley:

After twisting for hours through the Italian Alps, getting cul-de-sacked in an unbelievable byway of old Perugia, and being rescued by a young magician who took the wheel and wormed us out to the high road, I feel psychologically ready to attempt a few comments in response to your question about academic freedom and the administrator. The subject is as exhausting as it is inexhaustible. The most I can do is try a few animadversions for your eye alone.

Academic freedom is something the top administrator is not supposed to understand but is expected to defend with his life. Probably the quickest way to distinguish between an academician and a "nonacad" is that the former, on this subject, will always begin, "I believe in academic freedom *and* . . ."; while the latter, assuming he has a modicum of sophistication, will begin, "I believe in academic freedom, *but*. . . ."

Having made this important distinction, I must begin this disquisition with "I believe in academic freedom, *but*. . . ."

In my judgment, it is one of the most abused, misused, misunderstood, and fragile concepts in higher education. It evolved as a necessary means of providing a small, intellectual elite with the protection needed to pursue a search for the truth in the public weal. It also provided an opportunity, under this protective mantle, for the promulgation of the truth as the seeker understood it. Presumably it was not unrelated to the idea of "benefit of clergy" provided by the Medieval and Renaissance church; but because this concept also is largely misunderstood, I will not complicate the sub-

29

ject by pursuing the analogy. Yet the ultimate purpose of academic freedom was not so much to protect the searcher after truth as to protect the public interest in freedom of inquiry and communication. In other words, society as a whole is the prime beneficiary, the professor and his student being only secondary.

There is no doubt in my mind, therefore, that one of the administrator's most sacred responsibilities is to protect and preserve academic freedom. Because he is the man who stands between the academy and the community, the exercise of this responsibility can be and frequently is quite painful. I think of an occasion some years back when, in an area heavily populated by individuals who had lost relatives or even personally suffered persecution under Hitler, I had to defend an invitation to the head of the American Nazi Party to speak on campus. As thoroughly despicable as I found everything for which the man stood, I felt nevertheless that the student group which issued the invitation had a right to hear him. Believe me, this was an aging experience, particularly in view of the fact that a large percentage of the faculty also seemed opposed to having Rockwell on campus. Sad to relate, I was and am still convinced that those who issued the invitation were not motivated by any desire for knowledge or truth but merely by a wish to create excitement. But you will learn as an administrator that you rarely can base decisions on your guess about the motives of other people— even though a prudent executive always takes them into consideration.

In another instance I was obliged to defend a dramatic production which with impunity could be described as pornographic. My task here was a little easier because, while there may have been some question as to the playwright's ability, in my mind at least there was none regarding his sincerity in seeking to express a certain kind of artistic truth. Further, the department attempted, albeit unsuccessfully, to limit attendance to serious students of the drama. A disaffected faculty member, however, alerted the press and the fat was in the fire.

These are the easy ones. As you will discover, if you pursue your ambition and assume a deanship or ultimately a presidency, there is always some individual or some group demanding that you seize the banner and storm the ramparts ahead of the troops—that you put your career or even your life on the line to fight for his or their particular objectives. One need not question their sincerity to remember the old maxim that a college president is a man who keeps his head while those around him are losing theirs.

The issue of academic freedom, however, is one on which the president must be willing to take a stand, regardless of cost. The first time I ever resigned a position—and I was fully ready for the resignation to be accepted—was when I discovered that the trustees had failed to renew a faculty member's contract on what, in my judgment, were absolutely unsound and unsupportable grounds, grounds which called into question the instructor's right to pursue the truth as he saw it.

The situation was far from simple, which is par for the course. To begin with, the trustees took their action precipitately without consulting even the president, let alone the dean—the position I then held. I was, in fact, on vacation when the instructor called me with the gladsome tidings. Their only explanation was that he espoused some points of view not in harmony with the traditional principles of the institution. This at least was quite true, but so did about half of the faculty. Further, none of us had been required to sign any pledge on appointment, nor was there anything in writing to suggest such a monolithic expectation. A new member of the board, however, a man who had passed his prime but who enjoyed the financial respectability which the college coveted, had expressed the kind of dissatisfaction with the young man which had obvious dollar signs on it.

My reaction was quick and decisive. I immediately wrote a very diplomatic letter to the board chairman indicating that the wisdom of the trustees was clearly sufficient to the needs of the institution, making the position of dean superfluous. So effective was my diplomacy that the executive committee held an emergency meeting, with me as star witness, and reversed its early action. Accordingly, my grateful children continued to eat. This sort of foolishness, of course, would scarcely be duplicated today when we have all adopted due process and operate under the threat of collective bargaining.

Academic freedom is a precious and vital principle; the trouble is that for this very reason it lends itself to all sorts of abuse. It is used, for example, to protect the weak and the incompetent, even the malicious and subversive. Perhaps the most bitter conflict within higher education today is between those who believe that the institution should be utilized for the preservation, extension, and promulgation of the truth and those who believe that it should be a staging area, and at the same time a sanctuary, for social revolution. Academic freedom was not intended for the protection of the violent and the nihilistic. If, as I am afraid is increasingly the case, they preempt its protective mantle while sallying forth with drawn swords, academic freedom as such is on the way out. There is no question that the public is long-suffering and tolerant, but there is evidence of growing impatience with the use of academic freedom for purposes for which it was not designed.

You might well ask, then, why the academic community does not do something about the matter. I can answer only that we are caught in our own inconsistencies, hung up on our own shibboleths, hoisted by our own petards. All this metaphoric flight implies is that the professoriat itself is rather easy prey to those who consciously or unconsciously use academic freedom for inappropriate ends. The problem may well be that our traditional stance calls for detachment, for viewing both sides of every issue. Thus we find it as difficult to detect sinister intent as to accept commitment. More likely, the problem stems from the fact that too many have allowed too few to interpret the meaning of academic freedom for them. We have not worried it through for ourselves. We thus become apprehensive and arm ourselves for battle whenever anyone else so much as hints that his freedom is being infringed. So we tolerate the most incredible kinds of inefficiency and unprofessional, at times perhaps even immoral, conduct because we fear taking an action that might deprive a colleague of his traditional right to total self-determination.

Moreover, even though we still do not accord instant tenure, we as a profession provide instant academic freedom the moment an instructor enters the classroom for the first time. Unless and until academic freedom, like tenure, becomes something that has to be earned; unless and until the profession sets certain realistic limits upon the extension of academic freedom; unless and until each professor is required to be accountable for the exercise of such freedoms, both academic freedom and the academic community are in the gravest danger. Our very idealism becomes our worst enemy.

And on this cheery aphorism I start out on the road toward Rome. I hope you have observed that this discussion of academic freedom totally eschewed the word "responsibility." Let me say only that those who would use the first wisely will accept the second gladly.

Yours,

C. J.

Dear Stanley:

Rome's creative energies, which once went into imitations of Greek art and the science of politics, seem now to be capsuled in small four-wheeled cannisters manipulated by maniacs. The attendant chaos takes me back to an evening many years ago when I had to sit through several hours of freshman skits. Only one of them was remotely memorable. It pictured a harried neophyte complaining to the dean about the confusion he experienced during registration. "Young man," said the dean, drawing himself up in full dignity, "do you think for a moment it was not planned that way?"

Which brings me to the subject of administrative style. Some administrators seem to encourage chaos so long as (to borrow from Winston Churchill) they can control it. Obviously I do not commend this approach. In fact, when recruiting administrative staff I always try to ascertain if they are personally well organized; for if they are odds-and-ends individuals in their daily routine, they will very likely become so entoiled in minutiae that they will never get very much accomplished. The effect they will have on their colleagues, moreover, is much like that of a medical officer whom I served with in the army, a specialist in treating ulcers. He had plenty of practice. Everyone who worked with him had, or soon developed, one.

In my early days in administration I was very fond of the dean of a large division which enrolled as many as fifteen thousand students annually. He was kind enough to invite me to join his staff. By that time, though, I was entirely too familiar with his "Queen Bess" administrative style to wish to be part of his establishment.

34

Whether consciously or unconsciously, and I honestly never knew which, he surrounded himself with a half-dozen ambitious, very bright younger men, each of whom aspired to the position of right hand in the organization. Periodically one or the other would get the idea that the mantle was soon to fall upon his fortunate shoulders and he would work all the harder to make sure that there would be no slipups. But in the six years during which I had a chance to observe this operation rather closely, there never was a number two man! Moreover, there was never a clear or sharp delineation of duties and nobody knew exactly where he stood in the pecking order. (I seem to recall, without being in a position to check the source, that Henry Wriston, that maker of college presidents, expressly recommended keeping subordinates on their toes by refusing to define their several responsibilities!)

Although this style would certainly not be recommended in most administrative vade mecums, I must admit that in this particular instance it worked—despite a considerable cost to the psyches of the individuals concerned. Not many of them remained more than four or five years; but then administrators tend to be peripatetic under the most favorable circumstances, and their psyches are not infrequently considered to be expendable.

I would still much rather work for this type of man than for the "Inspector Lestrade" administrator who never allows anyone to do other than carry out orders under his constant surveillance. This sort of individual may be insecure himself and fearful that the mistakes of others will place him in jeopardy; or he may be a psychopathetic perfectionist who can't bring himself to believe that anybody else can do a job as well as he could himself. On the other hand, I have known a few of the breed who, superbly self-confident, operate in this manner because they like the sense of power it brings. One of these whom I worked with, an ex-military officer-turned-president, confronted the slightest error on the part of a subordinate with such vigor that his juniors not infrequently left his office quivering, even tearful. He was much admired, but not exactly loved.

The opposite style, total laissez-faire, can be sometimes effective too, but only if the second echelon consists of very skilled and loyal individuals. The best example I can recall from personal observation was the president of a large university who had had a distinguished career elsewhere but who had grown either bored or tired or both at his present institution. He rarely arrived in the office before noon and rarely left after one o'clock. Yet he lingered in the job for nearly two decades. In addition to his having two brilliant vice-presidents under him who quite literally ran the institution, for the most part without bothering to clear anything with him, he had a delightful and insouciant secretary. A favorite preoccupation of his, during his periodic visits to his office, was reminiscing to her about his earlier administrative experiences. On one of these interminable occasions she looked up at him with wide, innocent eyes and said, "Dr. Jones, aren't you glad you liv*ed* when you *did?*"

Despite such an exception, this administrative style rarely succeeds very long, and then only if, as in this instance, the second echelon is peculiarly able and trustworthy. These qualities are more difficult to come by than you might think; nor are they necessarily found in the same individual. As incredible as this may sound, I can record that one of the most brilliant administrative aides with whom I ever worked—and I would be happy to have him on my staff even now—told me quite candidly at the outset of our relationship that I should not rely on him too far. If there were ever a showdown in which his interests and mine were not consonant, I would be well advised to look sharply. I not only have no objection to this type of enlightened self-interest, but welcome it so long as it is accompanied by such candor.

I might digress here for a moment to offer a passing comment on the subject of loyalty in an administrative team. Obviously it is an essential ingredient for any kind of real satisfaction in the job. I have a certain sensitivity to this issue, for many years ago the loyal secretary of a man under whom I was serving charged me, when I made a critical comment about the boss, with being disloyal. Possibly I was. But my answer at that time, which would still be my answer, was that loyalty begins at the top. Unless an administrator gives thought to the welfare of those who are responsible to him he can scarcely expect them to feel any great loyalty.

Critical comments from a subordinate are, of course, to be expected. What matters is the audience to which the comments are addressed. Over and above the general ethical principle that one should not say behind a man's back what one would not be willing to say to his face (obviously a counsel of perfection!), I have the conventional "Whitehall" view that criticism should be kept inside the house. The counterpart, of course, is that within the house there should be complete freedom for dissent and argument. But what constitutes the house is not always self-evident; it must be defined clearly by the staff.

To return to the subject of loyalty, part of the price of its earning is the willingness of the top man to accept responsibility for shortcomings in his staff. A cardinal principle in the administrator's code is that the superior is responsible (and takes *explicit* responsibility) for the errors of his subordinates.

Assuming competence and honesty and loyalty, both above and below, the ideal style of administration would seem to be to delineate the broad areas of responsibility and then expect staff members to operate fairly independently so long as they are willing and able to make decisions and conscientious about keeping the dean or president informed.

This style of executive delegation calls for three special techniques if it is to be successful. First, it ideally involves a cabinet-type administration, with regular meetings so that lines of communication can be clear between and among the several echelons. Second, it requires a periodic review and reassignment of functions to make the most of the talents of the several administrators involved; and third, it calls for at least an annual written report and an accompanying evaluation, preferably discussed in the individual's presence.

I am sure that administration can be learned. As you know, there are a growing number of training programs in higher education which have achieved reputations for effectiveness. Withall, industry has gone well beyond higher education in the formal development of such training programs for the various administrative echelons. In the long run, however, I suspect that administrative

37

style is a function not so much of training as it is of character. And I have known some real characters in this business!

The Eternal City beckons.

Eternally yours,

Virgilius Coltswood

P.S. I can't go off to the Villa Borghese without still another observation. As you will discover, one of the great problems for a college or university president is to get information in such a way as to be able to act upon it with confidence. Since he perforce delegates many of his responsibilities to his chief aides, he tends to get his information as filtered through their minds. Whether consciously or unconsciously, however, most executives develop informal lines of communication. I have known these to become veritable systems of spies and counterspies. I think of one president who whenever he received an important report from a member of his staff would immediately call in someone else, even a sub-subordinate, and ask confidentially for a report on the identical subject. Needless to say, the news rather quickly got around. Needless to say, also, the end result was a general spirit of distrust in the whole administrative cadre.

Another individual whom I had occasion to serve with over a period of years, a financial vice-president, showed up at his office regularly every morning between five-thirty and six o'clock and met individually with groundsmen, janitors, et cetera—and the et cetera could include faculty members and students—in order to find out for his own use what was happening on campus. Through this means, he even managed on one occasion to get something on the president, or more specifically on one of the president's children, a lovely but rather impetuous, if not indiscreet, young thing who was enjoying her first experience with life in the raw.

Now do you see what I mean when I say that administrative style is a function of character?

C. J.

Dear Stan:

I have been thinking a little further since yesterday about this matter of style. It is not only a function of character but also of personality, and it manifests itself in a great many ways. There are cleric presidents who will wear their civvies when away from campus but when on home base would not be found dead in anything but formal black and round collar. At the other extreme is the president who could well afford a Savile Row tailor but who casually affects baggy tweeds with chamois patches even on the newest of elbows. Perhaps the most colorful president on the scene as of this writing is a man who not only wears a multicolored tam but whose PR staff has distributed hundreds of them to other dignitaries all over the countryside.

The old tradition calls for fairly conservative dress on the part of the president. Attendance at one national meeting is enough to show how persistent this tradition is. On the other hand, I have known presidents, and confess to being a bit guilty of this myself, who deliberately affect garb several degrees more peacockish than that normally worn by their associates off and on the campus.

This matter of dress, to be sure, is rather trivial, but it does lead into the broader and more serious subject of the president's public relations. He is, after all, the symbol of the institution. No matter what he says or does reflects upon its image. So long as he holds the office, the President of X College is the President of X for every moment of his life when he is visible to anybody outside of his own immediate family. He can never act publicly in an "unofficial" capacity because no possible disclaimers can prevent people from thinking of him as the President of X.

Incidentally, this imposes a heavy psychic burden on the president's family as well. They, and especially his wife if he is lucky enough to keep one, may be his only real confidante—the only audience with whom he can really let himself go. But this entails a derivative obligation of discretion for her as well. Caesar's wife must be above reproach! (Possibly this area of family involvement would justify a separate letter. Mary, please note!)

The president must, therefore, give the matter of his personal public relations much more than a passing thought. If he is fortunate enough to have a good PR man, one in whom he has confidence, he should discuss the matter of his personal image vis-à-vis that of the university thoroughly enough to make certain that the former is supportive of the latter.

Quite obviously, the problem changes as the needs of the institution vary. In a tax-supported college in the midst of a large metropolitan area, where students and faculty are drawn from a wide geographical reach and where local financial support is relatively unimportant, the president very likely can afford to give only a minimal amount of attention to his external image. On the other hand this kind of institution is rarer than its presidents may think. (The only president I know to have joined a protest march was rather short lived in office.) The more usual pattern calls for a deliberate and self-conscious approach to the presidential image; and, as I just implied, this statement also includes the presidential wife.

With more than a slight amount of self-consciousness, let me tell you about the approach we took when we assumed our first presidency—and by we, I am being neither editorial nor royal but purely domestic. The college had reached a fairly high level of academic respectability. On the other hand, in its immediate service area it was still, in the minds of a great many people, the place where they should send their children as a last resort. The fact that its educational program was far better than many that enjoyed greater prestige merely indicated how difficult it is for the image of a college to change. One of our alumnae actually confessed to me that, when she applied for membership in the Junior League, she was advised not to put down that she was a graduate of our college.

With a great many things working in our favor, we set about to create a different image. First, we emphasized the fine and performing arts and, through a stroke of good fortune, managed to obtain for a period of several weeks one of the outstanding collections of the day—with a champagne opening, by invitation only. Further, aided by the exceptional skills of my social secretary and helpmeet, we early on held a series of dinners, at some of which we expected formal attire. This even included an annual stag dinner— gourmet menu, black tie, the works. Through such devices, even on a modest budget, we managed to bring about important modifications in the traditional image of the college. With a degree of ingenuity, moreover, nearly all of these activities proved ultimately to be self-supporting.

Turning now to a seemingly unrelated aspect of administrative style, I would like to comment on the president's public utterances, starting with the obvious suggestion that it helps if he is reasonably articulate and literate. Americans consume speakers the way whales do plankton, and every new college and university administrator is immediately and tremendously in demand.

It has been my practice for the first year or two in every new position to respond to as many requests for speaking engagements as possible, provided that a fair-sized audience is available. If I speak to a small group it must be a representative or significant group. Only under the rarest of circumstances, moreover, do I deliver either a "canned" or an extemporaneous speech. Equally, very seldom will I speak more than a half hour. The knowledge of when to stop is the rarest jewel in any speaker's diadem.

At the end of two years I become conscious, or my wife and secretary begin subtly and then not so subtly to suggest, that a saturation point has been reached; whereupon, despite the fact that many college and university presidents pride themselves on the number and variety of speeches they make, I become highly selective and rarely commit myself to more than one major address a month.

The circumstances obviously determine the selectivity. When

I was associated with a church-related college I spoke to a number of church groups. At any institution, private or public, the president should try to make the alumni circuit once every two years. He and his top aides would do well to speak with some frequency to service clubs and to public school organizations, for these have considerable significance in determining community attitudes. It is also a good idea to make a kind of "annual report" to a few key service clubs so that they can be kept abreast of institutional developments as seen through the eyes of the president. With a little planning, he can ensure the presence of the news media.

One question which relates to this matter of public speaking is whether or not to require an honorarium. In general, an administrator's duties include public relations and therefore an honorarium may represent a form of double compensation. On the other hand, many organizations, including service clubs, pay out-of-town speakers but would never dream of compensating someone from the local college or university. Since we are a society that seems to appreciate things more if we pay for them, there are many situations in which the administrator has every right to want to be appreciated. I know one university president who requires an honorarium for every public address he delivers but indicates that the money goes into a scholarship fund which he has established in the memory of his deceased daughter.

There is another way, too, to look at this matter. Even though public speaking may be a part of the administrator's expected duties, very few of us are so endowed with staff that we are able either to have our speeches ghostwritten or to afford the luxury of time to prepare them during the working day. Therefore they come out of our few precious free evenings or even more precious weekends. Until the day comes when the president is offered time and a half for overtime—and I hope this day will never come—he should let an easy conscience be his guide as to whether he wishes to be a paid or a non-paid performer.

My rambles bring me now to a more perplexing philosophical issue: whether or not the president should take stands on public issues. He quickly finds that all sorts of groups seek his active and vocal support. Nevertheless he is technically the spokesman for the entire institution, not for a single component thereof. Further, regardless of pious disclaimers, whatever he says in public is interpreted as the official policy of the institution. Thus he finds himself caught in a familiar dilemma. If he takes no stands, he is considered by some to be either wishy-washy or a man without convictions of his own. If he takes stands, he is likely to offend significant portions of his constituency.

Each administrator, of course, develops his own style in this matter. Being a basically cautious individual, it has been my practice to take public stands only on issues which appear to me to have an important bearing on the welfare of the college and, even then, only on my own initiative. On the surface this sounds like a reasonable and rather simple resolution. In practice it is anything but. For example, the use of marijuana is still an issue of importance to a substantial segment of the students and faculty; and considering the degree of use of marijuana by college-age youth and the sharp public reaction thereto, this would appear to be an important educational issue. Despite strong personal views on the subject, however, I would not voluntarily take a public stand for or against it except to point out that the individual who elects to smoke marijuana should also be ready to endure the consequences. (On the other hand, I would not hesitate to call publicly for a review of the laws governing its use.) Conversely, on any issue, such as proposed legislation, affecting academic freedom I would feel compelled to speak.

The problem, as I see it, is that the college president must be highly selective in the issues which he elects to support or oppose. Otherwise he will be expending precious energies which could be devoted more profitably to other subjects and he might even find himself prostituting the dignity of his office.

This letter is too long already, but there remains one final phase of this rather wide-ranging subject of presidential style on which I must comment. I am thinking here of his relations with the news media, in which I include also the campus newspaper. If he is extremely fortunate, he can ignore the media and they will ignore him; but this is highly unlikely now that education is not only our national religion but our principal spectator sport. As I sat this afternoon in the Roman Coliseum watching the hundreds of cats and the thousands of tourists watching the hundreds of cats, I could not help wondering how much of that structure would have been necessary if the Romans had had the distraction of a passel of colleges and universities in the immediate environs!

My best advice on dealing with the media is to get a good PR man and let him handle the whole affair. Never speak directly to a reporter unless he has been cleared through the PR man or unless the latter is present. Never seek personally to correct a misquotation, and never answer any challenge. And when a statement is clearly called for, try to snatch sufficient time to write it out carefully in advance. Usually, even for a press conference, a good PR man can arrange to obtain most of the questions in advance. Despite all these precautions, I assure you there will be times when you will be caught napping or off guard. The only thing you can do then is pray that your reporter has had a good night's sleep. If he has not, you may not have one either.

But I am going to have one tonight, unless the Roman spaghetti and red wine decree to the contrary. Tomorrow we are off to Florence and the Renaissance man.

Vale,

C. J.

Dear Stanley:

When a derelict student of the Renaissance visits Florence for the first time, he experiences a certain welling up which must be shared with any who will listen. Thus you can understand the tremendous restraint I am exercising at the moment as I force myself to stick to the general theme of our correspondence. Highly commendable of me, what!

A recent issue of the *International Herald Tribune,* which I just came across this morning, contains an article by Russell Baker, in his usual acerbic style, on the subject of the university president's power. In the same edition Joseph Alsop comments on student uprisings at Harvard. There are in addition two editorials on campus unrest and several news items on disruptions on various college or university campuses. To top it off there is a dramatic picture of a distinguished member of the SDS at Columbia University posing in an open window, brick in hand, ready for "dialogue" with the administration. All of these in a very real sense relate to the subject of presidential power, or the lack thereof.

For decades now—ever since the decline and fall of the old presidential monarchic system—the campus head has been so increasingly powerless that the various recent utterances by politicians and pundits on his ineffectuality seem almost redundant. On the other hand, I have not shied away from redundancies in my previous letters and am not inclined to do so in this. For there are subtleties in the matter of presidential power which I have yet to see discussed by any of the learned commentators. I propose, therefore, to record some random thoughts.

Last spring when I had the pleasure of appearing with two of my fellow presidents before a hostile legislative committee investigating certain alleged campus obscenities, we were enjoined to declare who was in fact running our campuses. Because the situation clearly required it, I asserted without hesitation that *I* was running *my* campus. Since only a few weeks earlier one of our faculty members reportedly told a receptive coterie of his fellows that the president really had no power, I made my declaration with a few unvoiced reservations.

At about this same period, and on at least three occasions since, I have met with congeries of militant students who presented their "demands," giving me a generous interval of hours in which to meet them or else. In every instance the demands were "unnegotiable" and, what is more important for this discussion, they were presented to the president alone, without the comforting presence of his staff. Although my aides were near at hand and willing, the students refused to discuss the issues with anyone except the president, in solitary majesty.

What we have here is a curious contradiction, a paradox of conflicting evaluations. Certain of the faculty, on their part, are fully persuaded that the president has, and should have, little or no power. Certain militant student groups, on their part, see him as the omnipotent father image who has merely to press a button to right all wrongs. Their resentment is thus directed against him because in their perception he refuses, when he does, out of mere caprice—or, what is worse, moral indifference—to create the perfect academic society. (I will accept the possibility, of course, that they may actually have a fairly realistic appreciation of his situation and, as a mere matter of tactics, choose him as their target because of his pivotal, and exposed, position.) But whatever the student expectation, recent academic history contains example after example of administrative responses to campus disruptions which have been rendered ineffectual by failure of the faculty at large to reinforce presidential authority.

Nor does the dilemma end here. The historian of this period will find that many top public officials demand rigorous response

by college administrators to campus disturbances. Yet when viola-
tors are brought to court, their cases are often treated with anything
but firmness. What is more, certain well-meaning national organizations give the appearance at times of going out of their way to
provide encouragement to students who resort to violence in order
to bring about change. The college president and his staff are ineluctably caught in the middle.

My first inkling of this administrative dilemma came many
years ago when campus problems were so simple that I cannot help
reflecting on those as the halcyon days. As dean of a small college
and as the official who, under long-standing policies, had been delegated responsibility by the faculty to maintain discipline, my worst
problems were panty raids, water fights, bacchanalian orgies, and
so forth. That was the same period when the president of Princeton
University was quoted in the press as responding to a rather destructive campus disturbance with the startling observation, "Youth
will be youth!"

The particular episode which I recall from my own experience began with an innocent water fight between two fraternities
and gradually developed into a full-scale melee. The dean of students had disappeared for the evening, and I had to move into the
fray. The local police, at my pleading, agreed to give me fifteen
minutes to restore peace and order. Dodging water-filled missiles,
I charged into the two fraternity houses, identified their officers, and
directed the participants immediately to cease and desist. Either
through unwillingness or inability, the student officers failed to restore order; whereupon the police and fire departments moved in.
At this point things really got out of hand, and ultimately some
thirty dripping combatants ended up in jail. Came the morning and
I, acting within my authority, placed both fraternities on a six-week
probation, during which period they were denied all social activities. Came the evening and the faculty, in plenary session and operating within its authority, blithely reversed my order. Thereupon, in
righteous pique, I declared that I was returning to the faculty at
large the responsibility and authority for campus discipline it had
delegated to me.

47

But those were simpler times and simpler issues. More recently we have seen the development of such organizations as the SDS, which has as its avowed purpose the fomenting of disruption and even insurrection on the campus. The public rightly insists that these activities be sternly repressed. Such responsible national bodies as the American Council on Education, the Association of American Colleges, and the American Association of University Professors have come out with declarations that disruption and violence are totally unacceptable. And yet almost daily we read of new disruption and violence, with the president always the man in the middle.

Thus the issue of presidental and administrative power becomes increasingly important in higher education. I am not surprised to find Joseph Alsop, whose views I can normally take or leave, predicting that either authority must be restored to the administration or chaos will take over.

What is more—and I certainly lack the prescience to foretell the outcome—our campuses are reflecting to a high degree the polarization of society at large as between those who seem to demand total freedom and those who would be satisfied with nothing less than an almost dictatorial control. And the president, as never before in academic history, can satisfy no one.

I would not like to conclude this lighthearted disquisition with the impression that the president has *no* authority. You are doubtless aware of Clark Kerr's prediction that the chief administrator will ultimately be little more than a consensus taker. This ties in with the presidential model, so often held up by certain faculty philosophers, of the rector in a European university, the amiable amateur who is elected by his colleagues to serve usually for a very limited term. That this system is satisfactory is, I believe, both a misconception and a delusion; and as you know, Stanley, part of the purpose of my present busman's holiday in Europe is to find out about it for myself.

In a subsequent letter I want to talk about student power. For the moment it is enough to say that students come and go and therefore should not be permitted to make the ultimate determination concerning the future of the institution. The permanent body within most academic communities is the faculty, which gains its permanence through the tradition of academic tenure. It might seem logically to follow that the faculty should exercise the ultimate authority, as has so often been argued. On the other hand, the very existence of permanent tenure means that the faculty cannot be held ultimately responsible, since there is no effective instrument for the enforcement of accountability. Presidents, vice-presidents, and deans can be removed if they exercise their authority irresponsibly or ineffectively. Thus, to the extent that accountability and responsibility go together, the ultimate authority should be placed in their hands.

The administration, however, does not exist to exercise authority. In the long run its function is to provide a climate on campus where learning can most effectively take place. No blatant display of presidential power has ever yet created such a climate. Granted, in times of crisis not much else can create such a climate either. But regardless of what may appear in the charter and by-laws, the authority of the president, his real leadership, depends upon the willingness of the campus to accept him as its leader. If it will not, well there are other ways for him to make a living.

You may wonder, Stanley, what got me so wound up when this visit to Florence should really have provided another kind of stimulation. My best explanation is that I bought today a lovely edition of Machiavelli's *Il Principe* and also, at around sundown, stood on the spot near where they burned Savonarola!

Yours in the heat of the moment,

Charles

49

Dear Stanley:

It's not easy in this lovely corner of the Italian Mediterranean to think of anything, let alone the intricacies of university administration. But I shall turn my face to the wall and try.

Among the other problems related to the president's waning power which deserve a few reactionary comments are those having to do with faculty recruitment. In the old days, and perhaps still in a few small colleges, the president was the chief recruiter. I can recall a long-time estrangement between the president and the chairman of an English department based on the former's alleged unilateral hiring of a faculty member who first became known to the department when he appeared at the opening day of class in the fall. In truth, he was hired to fill a vacancy occurring during the summer, at a time when the chairman was gallivanting somewhere in Wordsworth country and no one else from this small department was around.

Faculty recruitment was for many academic generations the exclusive prerogative of the president, giving rise to the definition of a great university as the long shadow of a great man. Without a significant role in recruitment, the president has certainly a very limited opportunity to determine the course of his institution. To illustrate, in a distinguished liberal arts college in the East, in the late forties, the president and dean conceived a major academic departure which had the effect of revolutionizing the college and ultimately advancing it into the first rank. Taking advantage of their significant involvement in recruitment, and without discussing the program with the faculty, the two administrators made certain

50

that every new instructor was likely to be sympathetic with their concept. This procedure clearly involved much more than a perfunctory interview with the candidate. At the end of four years, with a clear majority, the president and dean proposed their new program to the faculty and received overwhelming support.

In another small college in the Midwest the president used to boast that he interviewed every prospective candidate by taking him for a long walk in the woods. While we might question whether such sylvan preoccupation represents a particularly scientific personnel procedure, it certainly enabled the participants to discover whether they were sympatico. An evening in a pub might do the same!

The problem in the large university, of course, is much more complex. In one institution where I served, the annual replacements and additions totaled in the hundreds. In such a situation it would be impossible for the president to interview all candidates. But the physical dimension is not the only complication. A philosophy has developed among faculties that only a faculty member is able to judge the desirability or competence of a potential colleague. Regardless of how many decades the president or dean may have taught before falling from grace, he presumably suffers some kind of "sea change" the moment he moves from the one power structure to the other. My first recognition of this came when I was still rather new in this intellectual limbo. As panel chairman for a regional meeting of academic deans who were to discuss "effective teaching," I surveyed my faculty colleagues for opinions on the subject. Virtually the first response I received was the acerbic query, "What can a dean know about effective teaching anyway?" My reply, if I had bothered to make one, would have been that if he does not know a great deal about it, he should seek some other means of gainful employment.

Except for instances where a really controversial figure is proposed for the teaching staff, the professoriat and even the trustees seem increasingly to think that hiring should be the almost exclusive prerogative of the faculty. This concept is further encouraged by practical considerations of finance. Faculty, not administrators,

51

attend the annual meetings of their disciplines (although at one point in my career I was actually invited by a department to go along to the annual convocation so that I could interview while the members attended meetings). Since these meetings constitute the principal "slave markets" for faculty recruitment, the temptation to combine recruitment funds with funds for professional improvement for the faculty is almost irresistible. Thus the dean or president, if he is involved at all, plays a very limited role in recruitment—except in the very last stages and possibly even then only by exercising a veto.

It would be absurd for any president to pretend that he is sufficiently conversant with all of the disciplines to judge a potential faculty member's competence. On the other hand, in view of the high degree of specialization involved in so many academic disciplines these days, it may be equally absurd to assume, for example, that a physical chemist can really judge the competence of a biochemist. Thus it is almost as irrational to assume that the administration should make all such decisions as it is to assume that the individual departments should do so exclusively. Nevertheless, in many large universities and in some small colleges as well, the prerogative has passed from the office of the president or dean to the department, with the chairman serving merely as the ballot counter.

One result of this procedure is that weak departments tend to become weaker and one-sided departments to become more one-sided. In an area such as psychology, where there are distinctly warring schools of professional thought, the majority vote will always result in the hiring of someone sympathetic with the majority approach to the subject. I have observed "creativity" art departments which, over a period of time, have almost totally weeded out the faculty members who believe in the more traditional "mastery-of-technique" approach; political science departments which hire only Democrats; economics departments which are totally unsympathetic to the capitalistic system; and I hesitate even to mention English or philosophy departments in this context! Moreover, departments which contain no productive scholars are unlikely to add to their ranks someone whose interest in research will make the elder statesmen look bad. Departments and schools of education throughout the country are particularly susceptible to this kind of skewing. For this reason, reforms in the preparation of elementary and secondary schoolteachers almost invariably come from without rather than from within.

Another difficulty which is almost inevitable in this process is that politically oriented departments tend to hire controversial faculty members because of their controversial nature rather than because of their knowledge of or dedication to the particular discipline. That this accusation would be stoutly rebutted is almost axiomatic. The president, who in point of fact has little power to contravene such appointments, is the one who must accept the brunt of criticism from within and without. Yet a word of caution is needed here, for there are controversial faculty members who are indeed competent in their field and in their profession. In these instances the president may well have to put his reputation on the line, as I observed in an earlier letter, to protect our academic freedom.

One accommodation to the quantitative realities which seems rather widely accepted is that appointments in the two lower ranks in larger institutions are generally made without reference to the central administration. New appointments to the rank of associate and full professor may still require active presidential or vice-presidential approval. In theory this provides some safeguards. In practice it still leaves much to be desired. A controversial instructor right out of graduate school can be just as damaging to an institution (or in a few instances just as helpful) as a controversial full professor. But refusal to accept a departmental recommendation at any level can be so traumatic that only the most foolhardy dean or president seems willing to take the risk. On the other hand I do not advocate a return to the old system of total presidential authority. The only feasible approach is for a united effort based on mutual trust and understanding—which proves, Stanley, that I too believe in miracles.

As at least a minimal accommodation, I would advocate

that every department be required to inform the responsible school and university officials of irregularities in the background or experience of the prospective faculty member. For example, all gaps in employment should be identified and explained. If a man has moved around too frequently, this should be evaluated along with the recommendations. Disciplinary actions or problems with legal authorities should not be glossed over. Letters of recommendation from chairmen and professors should be supplemented by records of at least one or two direct phone inquiries with administrative officers from the individual's previous institution or institutions. And finally, because the new faculty member is not only a member of his department but a member of the overall faculty, I would have a faculty-elected, schoolwide committee review all departmental recommendations before any commitment is made. As I indicated, Stanley, my views are somewhat reactionary!

I realize that the tone of these comments suggests a deliberate attempt on the part of many departments to put something over. Unfortunately, this does happen. More often, however, the problem is simply the lack of sophistication on the part of many faculty groups and even departmental chairmen. Also, during those periods when the market is extremely competitive, the department frequently may be motivated by a felt necessity to fill a position rather than to obtain a fine teacher and scholar. Thus, if we are to preserve institutional integrity, I see no alternative to having an effective partnership in recruitment—with ultimate administrative control.

Brief, to the point, and quite out of harmony with this exquisite setting, and perhaps even with the times!

As ever,

C. J.

54

Dear Stanley:

There is probably one thing only which should be brooded upon in a scene as lovely as this and that is the luxury of time, a luxury college administrators generally think they cannot afford. For the first time in thirty years I can afford it, but old habits are hard to lay aside! I have heard more than one administrative colleague complain that he has not been able to take a vacation in x years, the x standing for anything from three to fifty. Would that I were so indispensable!

Only this morning I received a letter from home—home for a college president is where he hangs his mace—with the distressing news that one of my two top aides has been demobilized for three weeks with a condition described as "acute fatigue." Little wonder! I have been after him for years to take a real vacation. He has continuously promised me that he would, yet in all that time he never has.

This is not to say that he never took extended periods, say two weeks, from the office; but energetic and devoted as he is, he always found his services quickly in demand for other concerns. And when these, by some miracle, were not immediately in evidence, he assigned himself energetically to his family and home. I understand that such a character in some quarters is known as a workaholic. I mention this not out of the slightest lack of respect. He is, in fact, a quite remarkable person; and when the scroll is unfurled up yonder I have little doubt that his name will be second only to that of Abou Ben Adam.

I perforce speak selfishly. At a time when I seriously need

him to keep shop his neglected batteries have decided finally to seek their own means of recharging. Thus I suggest, not frivolously, that your very first question when you are interviewed for admittance into the mysteries of administration should concern the vacation schedule. Start by demanding all the normal vacation periods accorded students and faculty, plus six weeks in the summer and four additional weeks just before the spring solstice. You will not, of course, get all of this, but if you are concerned with a long life and a merry one there is no harm in trying.

At one private university where I served, the president was adamant in insisting that he and his vice-presidents get completely away from college duties for four or five days each six weeks. Generally I contrived to save a few credits for a two-week respite on a favorite Caribbean isle, one preferably without telephones. This kind of soul-serving is more difficult, of course, at state colleges and universities where all staff members are public employees, with the president being slightly more so. Even when he can get away, he has become so accustomed to phone calls beginning with "I am a taxpayer and I demand . . ." that a vacation without one such call would probably make him uneasy.

I have never, however, in thirty years of administrative work failed to take my regular summer vacation, usually an uninterrupted four weeks. The first two are spent in licking my wounds, the third in thoughtless exuberance, and the fourth in gearing for the excitement which inevitably awaits my return to campus. Moreover, I have generally contrived successfully to place at least one thousand miles between me and the office. Although this rarely means no calls at all, it certainly restricts both their frequency and their duration.

Since I believe I can still get another page or two in the envelope without adding another thousand francs in postage, I shall ramble on to where the last remark leads me. Still on the question of your vacation, let me assert quite positively that the real test of any presidential secretary is the mail she refuses to forward to her vacationing boss. Third-class mail should be dispatched at once to the library or, better yet, placed in the circular file; second-class mail should be stored quietly in some deep recess far removed from the presidential desk. As for first-class, all bills should be held unless they contain the threat of exorbitant overdue penalties. Hints that they may be turned over to a bill collector may safely be ignored.

But there is virtually no correspondence concerned with the university that cannot be answered with a promise to "bring it to his attention immediately on his return" or handled by some other administrative officer. As any good secretary knows, the best way to diminish the salutary effects of a vacation is to confront her office charge immediately upon his return to his desk with a large stack of unanswered mail. Mine—blessed creature that she is—has a way of accumulating just enough on my desk to make me feel important and missed, but not enough to create instant depression. Curiously enough she always manages to discover a few additional folders as day follows day, thus easing me into the familiar routine. Even these, however, she has carefully divided, not chronologically, but into categories by degrees of urgency. At which point I am reminded of the old saw in British civil service: "Leave the file long enough in your in-tray, and you can take the green [urgent] label off."

I do not mean to sound irreverent concerning the bane of every administrator, the daily deluge of mail. Often, despite my assistant's preliminary efforts, I feel that I am little more than an overpaid routing slip. I get rid of every letter I can possibly send to someone else on the staff, either requesting him by appropriate checks on the routing slip to answer directly or to prepare a letter for my signature. My secretary always makes a note of the latter so that reminders can be sent along after a month or two of inactivity. *But*—and here I state one of the very important rules in my personal administrative praxis—only in the rarest of circumstances will I fail to reply to a letter addressed to me in my official capacity. I suspect, in fact, that I am obsessive on the subject, but I have not found any rational ground for changing a practice learned in my very first administrative post. On the other hand, I have never been able to live up to another rule in that early office, which was that the letter had to be answered within twenty-four hours unless its content required more time for assembly or analysis.

In pursuit of this laudable requirement in those ancient days,

I remember responding to a series of letters and cards from a certain individual making inquiry about such fascinating topics as the meaning of the University's Latin motto (one of the professors of classics assured me that it was untranslatable) and the reasons why the third chancellor failed in his efforts to move the campus to what was at the time a suburban area. Because I had a few other responsibilities I was beginning to feel a little impatience with this question-and-answer game, a fact which I relayed one day at lunch, card in hand, to our alumni secretary. Whereupon the good gentleman nearly collapsed into his Irish stew; for he immediately recognized my correspondent's address as that of a nearby mental institution. I will add only that thereafter I ignored all letters and cards from a certain Mr. E., treating them as we did our "crank" mail by forwarding them to the chairman of the department of psychiatry.

I learned another thing in those early years about office routine. In view of our mutual heritage I need scarcely remind you of the innate parsimony of the Dutch, be they the Holland or Pennsylvania variety. I could never see, for example, making three copies of all letters, including enclosures, when all we really needed was one original and one file copy. One frenetic morning I personally hunt-and-pecked an impatient enclosure to be sent with a letter to the chairman of the board of trustees, without making so much as a single copy. And the original became lost in the delivery! Believe me, Stanley, no economy is worth such a contretemps. Remember, never less than an original and two, even of your own doyenish doodles!

The basic administrative theory underlying all this is that nothing is official unless it is in writing, and if one person has it in writing you had better be sure that all parties concerned have it as well. The resultant avalanche of paper is a miniscule hazard as compared with the Scylla of despair in not being able to produce an official copy at the right moment. I recall a particular letter in which I laid down certain grim demands to be met by a member of my administrative staff. He did not meet them, and when the deadline arrived and I was about to suggest that he seek other areas of service for his remarkable talents, we could not find anywhere a copy of

58

my letter putting him on warning. I know now that any letter of such importance should be sent via registered mail with a return receipt requested. In this instance it took nearly two more years to accomplish the divorce which should have come with a simple pull on a filing-case drawer.

From vacations to long-distance lines to filing cases may seem almost as far as from cabbages to kings, but it is simply that sort of day. A mistral seems to be moving in, which suggests that I should be brief—a note on which I will end. For despite this discursive letter, Stan, and if you forget all the other gems of advice contained herein, remember to be brief. One of my former colleagues, a man of considerable ability as well as commendable ambition, nipped his administrative career in the bud, I am convinced, because he was utterly incapable of saying anything with economy. His was a magnificent skill at elaboration, page after page of it, finely drawn and infinitely involute. But I hardly ever read anything he wrote to me or for me without recalling that cartoon in an old *New Yorker* in which a mother impatiently replies to a question from her little daughter by saying, "Go ask your father." "But," the child replies, "I don't want to know *that* much!"

And so, Stanley, to paraphrase Pascal et al., "If I had had more time, I should have written you a briefer letter."

Cordially,
Charles

Dear Stanley:

You may have noted that a substantial amount of our correspondence has gone under the bridge, or more precisely flown over the ocean, without my having given you any specific guidelines on how to become a college president—if you should decide to embark on such a rock-strewn course.

One way would be merely to have your title changed from something else, as happened to the president of the university at Aix-en-Marseille, with whom, as you can imagine, I spent an interesting and rather depressing two hours. His change of title from rector to president has not, I fear, added so much as a cubit to the power he needs to meet some of the crises with which he is now confronted. But don't let me get distracted from the purpose of this letter, which is basically a how-to-do-it exercise.

I would, in candor, have to admit that there are probably as many ways of becoming a college president as there are college presidents. Since there are at present an estimated three hundred presidencies going a-begging (no one really knows the actual count), it might appear as if there were about three hundred fewer ways than might actually be desirable in this bearish market! I may have a few moments at the end of this letter (because of the mistral 1 have loads of time this morning) to make a comment or two on how to *find* a college president; but suffice it to say at the moment that if similar tactics were used by search and rescue squads, the mortality rate would rise substantially. Of all the capricious, disorganized, unprofessional operations in human society, this one

60

would certainly appear to qualify for some kind of negative award, but more on that presently.

If I were a young man (and I wouldn't go through that again for anything) the first thing I would do is treat this presidential bug with the kind of microscopic analysis it truly deserves. In all likelihood, before it had an opportunity to exercise its virulent properties, I should drop it gingerly into a bottle of formaldehyde. But assuming that the soul-searching or the in-depth therapy left me still gazing eagerly up the administrative ladder, heedless of the admonition that at best it is a "splendid misery," I should begin the following preparations.

First off, I would get the doctorate, making certain that it was a PhD and not one of the several variants. The only thing to remember is that selection committees are ipso facto conservative, particularly if faculty participation is involved, and they are irrevocably convinced that the other doctorates signalize men of lesser abilities. I know two administrators of outstanding skills who were persuaded by their graduate adviser in a very distinguished university to take the EdD in preference to the PhD. Neither of these men has as yet achieved his goal of a college presidency, and I cannot but believe that the ill-advised choice of degree played some part in the frustration of their ambitions.

There is little doubt that receiving the degree from one of the very top graduate schools is preferable in the presidential competition. This too would appear to be rather absurd, particularly since graduate training as such has generally very little relevance to the college presidency. In your idle hours someday you might look at the doctoral origins of our current crop of presidents and let me know whether my impression here is valid.

Fashions do change, of course. When I took my doctorate, with an eye toward ultimately getting into college administration, the field of English literature seemed to be very much in demand. History and philosophy doctorates seemed also a good approach to college administration, possibly because there were many more graduates in these fields than available teaching positions. They had to get a job somewhere and so they went into administration. But

61

those were the olden days. Now we see chemists, economists, even MDs being handed the presidential mace.

I dare not risk letting my prejudices show by skipping over the possibility that a university presidency might go to a retired general, a successful minister, or an affluent banker. These good souls still occasionally catch the golden ring on the presidential merry-go-round and some of them have been good administrators. If student unrest, thoughts of which are inevitably lurking in the back room of any president's mind, continues apace, it may well be that our top academic administrators should hereafter be chosen from the ranks of the marines, the FBI, or the wardenate of the nation's correctional institutions. From the criticisms repeated almost daily in the press concerning the failure of our college presidents to put down student insurrection, it would appear as if those of us who have been extruded from the academic mill are qualified by neither training nor temperament for the prevailing battlefield conditions.

I must also, in scholarly fairness, comment very briefly on the growing number of doctoral programs which are specifically designed to prepare university administrators. Some of these are excellent. It is rare to find anyone in a student personnel function who has not had formal graduate preparation in the field. This is true as well for fiscal officers and increasingly true even for those who are concerned with buildings and grounds. On the other hand, as appropriate as many of these executive training programs are, it is still valid to say that relatively few officers on the academic side get their preparation through graduate study specifically designed toward that end. Something of a myth, I am sure, is operative here: that the most relevant preparation for a college or university presidency is a high degree of specialization in some academic discipline, specialization beginning in graduate school and carrying on through an extended period of classroom teaching and/or research. The training program for academic administrators at the University of Michigan reflects this myth, or better yet attempts to link it with reality, by providing a PhD which combines advanced training in a specific discipline with orientaton to administrative careers. In view of the importance of higher education, however, and the increasing difficulties of the presidential task, we may well find that the amateur, or for that matter the apprentice, approach to the complexities of administering a large academic organization will not long suffice. In the meantime, there is no particular evidence that the specialized programs for the training of university officials give the applicant any edge over his competition in the selection of a college president.

Either before or after the doctorate the aspiring college president should betake unto himself a wife. Her importance, if not otherwise obvious, was underlined by a study conducted a few years ago in which only two of several hundred college presidents surveyed (excluding religious celibates) were unmarried. Since all of the presidents' wives whom I know are ladies of infinite charm, marriage would seem to be one of the quintessential requirements. I hasten to add, though, that the lady should not be too glamorous. In the first place, the president probably could not afford to keep her adequately caparisoned; and in the second place, such a lady might well find campus life a bit confining. It helps, of course, if she has received a baccalaureate from one of the leading women's colleges, but I have known some very successful first ladies without so much as a single college degree. It is much more important that she count among her qualifications the ability to take a motherly approach to students and a fatherly approach to students' mothers. I would also recommend that she possess a few worldly resources, such as a pleasant annual income from the will of a favorite uncle and perhaps a cottage on a Grecian isle. Of her many other qualifications I could speak at length; but, to borrow a device from Laurence Sterne, I shall simply allow you the margins to fill with your own dreams. On the other hand, dear Stanley, let me say that I think your bride nicely fills all of these requirements—except that Grecian island. Also, Mary strikes me as a woman of infinite patience, a quality which both of you will find highly desirable in the next stage of this progress down the royal road to a college presidency.

Even though history records the names of a few brilliant administrators who moved into presidencies almost before they cut their eyeteeth, selection committees generally look for that kind of seasoning which only age can bring. So next comes the period when "ripeness is all." Since the president should be able to look any member of his faculty directly in the eye and say, in effect, "My academic qualifications are as good as yours," now is the time for him to devote his energies to a successful career in the classroom. He should strive for popularity with his students without lowering his standards of academic expectation. He should achieve the reputation of being liberal in his thinking but should at all costs avoid the appearance of being revolutionary in his actions. And above all he should be able to get along with his fellow faculty members, since any one of them might one day be able to put in a wrong word at the right time. Although the president ultimately must become a political animal, this is the period when he should devote his time to teaching and scholarly publication. But a caution here—he should not publish so much that he runs the risk of arousing jealousy on the part of his departmental colleagues. Rather he should aspire to "The Character of a Trimmer," exercising moderation at all times in all things. (I know a few notable exceptions here. One distinguished university president, long since retired, actually had an arrangement with his trustees providing several months annually for him to continue with his research and publishing.)

A young man of such virtues will doubtless be promoted rapidly in the ranks. By the time he is an associate professor of one or two seasons he should be ready for the next step, a step which must be taken most gingerly indeed. He must now manage to have himself appointed to one or two key campus committees, those dealing with curricular matters, faculty personnel, or long-range planning. On the all-college academic planning committee, he should espouse requests from the more powerful departments and occasionally come up with one or two ideas of his own. As a result and in due course he can expect to become a departmental chairman and later, with the right degree of maneuvering, an academic dean.

The deanship, of course, is the real testing ground; for here he must demonstrate a talent which up to this point he has wisely kept to himself—the ability to say "no" and not to give offense. Diplomacy requires that he consult with everybody on everything, but the time has now come for him to risk taking one or two unpopular stands just to indicate that he is his own man.

This is the stage in the aspiring president's career when he must achieve that all-important quality of visibility. Although he can point proudly to a half-dozen articles and a published book based on his dissertation, it is now essential that he begin addressing a varity of audiences on subjects far afield from his academic specialty. In this way he shortly begins to assume the aura of an academic statesman. He should also during this crucial period publish a few articles on subjects related to college and university administration, articles which display no small dash of humor to compensate for their probable lack of profundity.

He must also start attending regional and national meetings of such associations as the American Conference of Academic Deans, the Association of American Colleges, the American Council on Education, and so forth. Here, until he learns how successfully to avoid it, he will doubtless, to paraphrase Omar Khayyám, eagerly frequent doctor and saint and hear great argument but ever more come out by that same door wherein he went. Before cynicism sets in, he should take occasion to ask witty and penetrating questions, particularly in the smaller working sessions, so that shortly he may find himself with the opportunity of serving on a panel or two. But most of all, at these meetings he should work at knowing and being known. He will learn that there are "kingmakers" in this business, and without being too obvious he should make their acquaintance and try to get his name on their back-stair lists. Since these Earls of Warwick change from time to time, suffice it to say that the executive officers of the major associations are not infrequently consulted by search committees. There are even nonacademicians who function in the kingmaker role. Old John Amory Lowell, for example, is said to have directly picked six successive presidents of Harvard University, at a time when this post was second in prestige only to the presidency of the United States. Such a function is not infrequently played by the heads of the major philanthropic foundations, and the annual meetings of the academic associations often provide opportunity for becoming acquainted with these masterbuilders.

There is yet another reason for getting to know them. Our presidential aspirant must, somehow or other, receive one or two foundation or governmental grants, preferably for some idea relating to curricular or administrative improvement. Grants for research projects in his academic discipline are noted but are not necessarily relevant. For every search committee, even in tax-supported colleges, is impressed by the man who has a noticeable skill in the art of grantsmanship. It can well compensate for other shortcomings.

Now let us assume that the groundwork has been carefully laid. A good degree, a good wife, some brilliant teaching, some excellent research, a stormily successful deanship, and so forth. The time is now ripe to start looking. And incidentally, timing is of real importance. He should normally not leave the deanship in less than three years nor stay in it more than a half dozen without making a move, and move he should. An old friend of mine at the outset of my own career maintained, as I recall, that no ambitious man should settle down before he has changed positions at least three times. Since in our profession this probably also means a geographical relocation, he all the more needs a wife with stamina, the soul of a gypsy, and a modest patrimony.

Among other reasons why such moves are important, so long as they represent upward and not merely horizontal mobility, is that they provide a means for sharpening one's skills at handling interviews. Many a brave soul has been lost in the deep of not knowing how to conduct himself during the rigorous pleasantries of meeting with selection committees. Thus one should never overlook the opportunity to develop such skills by the expedient of pursuing every job offer, so long as the prospective employer is paying for the drinks.

I had occasion, Stanley, in an earlier letter to talk about getting things down in black and white. This is applicable in the interviewing process as well. I think of one time when I traveled a considerable distance to be interviewed for a position in which I was

66

only peripherally interested. I thought it understood that my expenses were to be covered. At the end of the interview, however, nothing was said, nor was the subject ever brought up again. My annoyance was somewhat compensated by my being spared a position which surely would have been something less than rewarding.

One of the presidential interviews I remember most warmly, even though I was not the successful candidate, began with the chairman's observation that the best way to get a line on a candidate was to permit him to ask the first question. His approach was, I believe, absolutely sound; and I have adopted this device many times myself. I am even rather proud of the question I asked on this occasion. The selection committee was exclusively comprised of trustees, and my question was simply, "What, gentlemen, would you do if I ended my first year with a deficit?" Since the immediate reply was, "This is precisely what we would expect if you were doing your job well," I have regretted ever since that they did not in their wisdom offer me the election.

I may have sounded a little crass a moment or two ago when I suggested that the aspiring president should not overlook any opportunity to develop expertise in interviewing. Let me correct this by saying that he equally should never waste the time of the devoted men and women who are seeking a president. This most important responsibility of a college trustee is usually assumed at no small personal sacrifice, and unless you feel a genuine interest you have a moral obligation to save his time and the institution's money. I recall one instance when I quite positively told the chairman, who had called me from the West Coast when I was living in the East, that I was not interested. He was quite insistent, however, believing that my interest might change after I visited the campus. He also mentioned the names of two people who had recommended me for the position, both of whom I respected highly. This, of course, added a dimension to my quandary, for if these men thought that the college and I may have been made for each other, I certainly had an obligation to put their judgment to a test. As it turned out, the interview was very unsatisfactory; for I found myself in the thick of what was evidently a philosophic difference of opinion between the trustee

67

and the faculty selection committees. As I recall, I subsequently received a half-dozen long-distance telephone calls from representatives of each point of view and even a call from the retiring president. As a result and with all the grace I could muster, I withdrew my candidacy.

It is ironical to me that, with hundreds of vacancies in college presidencies and perhaps thousands of interested and competent candidates, to date there is no adequate means of rendezvous. Although an increasing number of professional executive placement agencies are getting into the business, the fees charged for their services tend to discourage all but the more opulent colleges from turning to this resource. This is particularly unfortunate, for these agencies can provide a much more effective means of bringing about a satisfactory wedding than the hit-and-miss methods generally employed. One of their benefits is that they may preserve anonymity until the right candidate and the right institution appear ready to be introduced. In some ways, too, they can be a much better sales agency in soliciting the candidate's interest. But as yet theirs is only an expensive drop in the bucket in terms of filling the need.

Now that our fictional candidate has nearly reached his mark, I will close this letter with a few words of advice to selection committees, which you might wish to pass on when you yourself are in the throes of negotiation.

With a kind of absurd regularity, the announcement of a new presidential search or selection includes the statement that a "nationwide" exploration is to be made or has just been made. One implication of this remark is that colleges and universities, ignoring the practice of industry, seem to make little or no effort to prepare for administrative succession from within. While it is true that the retiring president should not ordinarily be able to pick his successor, it is equally true that there is something profoundly inefficient in a system that does not provide for preparation and selection from the ranks. The principal justification for not doing so is that universities often thrive on getting a new kind of leadership to meet the new requirements of institutional development. I think of one university which has had three presidents in its relatively short history. The first was basically a pioneer spirit, a man who was able to sell the community and service area on the idea of supporting a new institution for higher education. His successor was basically a builder, and during his successful term of office the campus was provided with a master plan and with buildings that were both attractive and commodious. But neither of these men was basically an educator and so the trustees deliberately set about to find someone to carry the institution, in its third stage, into greater academic respectability. All too often, the approach is merely to find the man in the hope that he will then present the institution with the proper direction. The more intelligent approach would be the reverse. And to me this is the strongest justification for participation of both students and faculty in the whole process of planning and search.

At least faculty should be involved to avoid the domination of a particular trustee or group of trustees. I recall one instance where the long-time chairman of a board had set his cap for a particular candidate. In executive session he informed his fellow board members that he would consider their failure to go along with him not only a vote of no confidence in his chairmanship but also a lack of appreciation for his many services to the college. He was both a wealthy and on the whole an intelligent man, and his contributions had indeed been many. The vote in behalf of his candidate had a majority of one. The resultant split in the board took many years to heal, and the new president, all innocently, had to work with one of the most deplorable of all handicaps, a divided board.

Whether more meaningful faculty participation could have averted this particular contretemps is hard to say. Another reason, however, for involvement of faculty is that the president is in effect primus inter pares. If his faculty colleagues have had some say in his selection, he enters his difficult position that much more secure.

Many of these same arguments apply to student involvement as well. In the last year the newspapers contained reports of at least two major university presidencies where the incumbent ran into serious and immediate difficulties because the student leadership felt that its views had been ignored by the trustees. In one instance the new president withdrew. In another he accepted the position but

69

encountered such student opposition that he resigned not many months later. This could well have been avoided if the trustees, while preserving their ultimate responsibility, had provided opportunity for genuine and meaningful participation on the part of both students and faculty.

What is often overlooked by selection committees is that the really good candidate needs to be sold the position. When he is brought to the campus for an interview it is not just he who is being looked over. If the schedule does not provide opportunity for him to meet with other members of the administration, men with whom he will have to work and on whom he must rely, he would be foolish indeed not to view the situation with some suspicion. Similarly, he should have an opportunity to talk with students and with members of the community, for these are people with whom he will have to relate and he should be able to get some feeling of the campus-community pulse before he makes so important a decision.

Also, far too few institutions provide funds to bring the candidate's wife to the campus. This is doubly foolish. They should certainly look the potential first lady over with care, for she is very much a part of the presidential retinue. Moreover, she should have a chance to determine whether or not she would find contentment in this new setting. I am aware of two instances in my administrative career when the president's wife, very shortly after the move, found the new setting so inhospitable that she refused to stay, with the most traumatic consequences. Since normally the president's salary represents a major investment, it is the greatest folly for the trustees to practice penury in the search and selection.

Well, Stanley, be tolerant of these musings. Normally it is not easy for the aspiring president to endure the elaborate process of seeking a satisfactory position. It is no less arduous for those on the other side of the search. But until some more satisfactory modus operandi is devised, these difficulties are likely to persist. Some years back I heard of a harried selection committee which, after two unsuccessful years, appealed to the distinguished president of a nearby university for advice. He urged them to stop looking for the knight in shining armor and content themselves with merely finding a pres-

70

ident. Perhaps this same advice is good in reverse. If you want to be a president, don't wait around for the ideal presidency. Just become a president.

And with that bit of pragmatism, I shall end this lesson and prepare to leave this charming old university town.

Au revoir,

C. J.

P.S.   If you still don't know how to find a presidency, perhaps the simplest solution would be to run an ad in the *Chronicle of Higher Education*. Others do it. Why shouldn't you?

Dear Stanley:

Before foraging for some of the delicious food for which Lyon is inexplicably noted (only beautiful cities should cater to gourmets), I feel moderately inspired to return to a subject on which enough can never be said. I refer to the president's own administrative staff, which, like a good secretary, can make or break him. They are in many ways more important than he, though their pay is not quite comparable. In short, he can probably afford to dine more often in a three-star Michelin resturant than can most of them—except possibly the chief financial officer and the head coach.

To start in an orderly fashion, one would first ask how many administrators are necessary. The best answer is the one I used to give my freshmen when they asked me how long a term report should be: "Just long enough." To some of the militant faculty members and to most state legislators, the answer would probably be a simple "none." From my years of experience in a variety of institutions as well as my services as an evaluator on eighteen or twenty different accreditation teams, I can say categorically that, Parkinson's Law to the contrary, I can think of no colleges and few universities where the administrative cadre has bodies to spare. But after all, this is an administrator speaking.

Because every college and university is different, I see little point in pursuing further the question of how many. A real concern of the president, however, should be to insure that no single administrative department (usually it is the financial area) gets an undue share of the total administrative budget. As a corollary to this, he would be wise to have some kind of understanding with an appropriate faculty committee to dispel the suspicion that faculty positions are utilized for administrative aggrandizement. An excellent safeguard, of course, is to encourage as many members of the administration as possible to teach an evening course, preferably without compensation, so that when the tally is made the instructional budget is seen borrowing from the administrative. What makes this balance all the more sensitive is that generally it appears as if administrators receive higher salaries than faculty members, an outrageous bit of favoritism! A study of Mark Ingram's book on administrative perquisites shows that the gap has been closing. Many administrators now get paid for a twelve-month contract about what their faculty counterparts receive for nine months. I won't bother commenting on the disparities in working hours, vacation periods, and the like.

Another very important concern is the number of individuals who are directly responsible to the president. As I recall, the British civil service contends that no administrator should have more than four people reporting directly to him. My own feeling is that the figure might go as high as seven, but only under the most compelling circumstances. Because of the increasing complexity of the president's assignment, many thoughtful observers of the administrative scene have contended that there should in fact be two presidents, or a chancellor and a president, a format already adopted by a few of our more forward-looking colleges and universities. In this arrangement the reporting will obviously depend upon the agreed division of duties. But one very important principle involved even here is that there should never be an unnecessary step in between administrative levels. Alongside this principle I would place a fact of life: to wit, there are always many more administrators who *feel* they should report directly to the president than he can possibly accommodate. As a result, one of the most successful ways to get rid of an undesirable administrator (a subject I shall touch upon further in a moment) is to rearrange the pecking order so that someone is between him and the official to whom he previously reported, particularly if he reported to the president. Still another effective way of achieving the same end is to institute such economies as to

73

force him to share a secretary when he has been accustomed to having his own—to have and to hold. But I get ahead of myself here.

Under ordinary circumstances—I can't think of even any extraordinary circumstances that would reverse this—the chief academic and the chief fiscal officer must report directly to the president. Even if the budget provides for an executive vice-president, these two must still have direct access to the top. If the college supports a development program (and which of us these days can afford not to?) the development officer should normally be in this same top echelon, as should, but here I speak slightly less ex cathedra, the public relations officer and the dean of students. As for the latter, in view of the student unrest on so many of our campuses, the best possible protection for the president is to have in this office a man whose responsibilities and authority are clearly evident throughout the academic community. Thus in recent years an increasing number of institutions have elevated this position to the vice-presidential rank.

There is frequently, in this ambitious colony, an almost endemic conflict between certain functionaries, such as the public relations officer and the development officer, each of whom feels he should be the vice-president, with the other reporting to him. Yielding to all such purely understandable self-aggrandizement would result in an administrative pattern where, as a rather earthy man with whom I worked once said, you can't throw away a cigar butt without hitting a vice-president. I have never seen an ideal solution to this problem. A development program cannot succeed without the support of a good public relations effort. The catch phrase is, I believe, "Not fund raising but friend raising." On the other hand both development and public relations contain quite discrete areas of responsibility and thus do not thrive well in a concentric relationship.

Once in my distant past I was the proud accumulator of three separate administrative titles, presumably in lieu of increases in salary. The question of administrative titles can at times become rather perplexing. In a large state system, where the central bureau provides an inflexible range of choice, the problem perhaps need not arise. Historically, every key administrator below the president wanted to be called dean. Long before this title had lost most of its decanal significance, the title of vice-president had become much more of a status symbol. The very useful title of secretary has pretty much fallen out of fashion, and while this was happening provost added its own element of confusion—a provost is a provost is a provost. . . . Inevitably paralleling academic ranks, the qualifying adjectives of assistant and associate were added to virtually every administrative rubric, including even that of president, though I have not as yet heard of a visiting or adjunct president.

I would caution you, Stanley, against ever becoming an "acting" anything. Acting presidents have been known to receive the unmodified symbols of office at the conclusion of a "nationwide search," but this happens all too seldom. The interregnum during which they hold responsibility without real authority normally plays havoc with their acceptability for the permanent post.

A not uncommon distinction is made between staff and line officers, presumably following the pattern of the military. Ideally, nearly every administrator should be an officer of the line: that is, a man with clearly defined responsibilities and authority. A possible exception is the assistant to the president, who can be tremendously useful depending on the role the president allows him to play. And to my own amusement, this has reminded me of another area of frequent conflict. I recall vividly one situation where the president's secretary set herself up successfully as the intermediary between the president and his assistant, a man of the highest professional qualifications. The president's office was known as "Fort Smith" after the name of the stalwart secretary. I have often wondered if this particular president ever knew what atrocities were committed in his name!

Every administrative budget should be sufficiently expansive for the president to have on his immediate staff a professional intern. One of the real tragedies in university administration in recent years, in my judgment, was the modification of the subsidized internship program sponsored by the American Council of Education

75

under a grant from the Ford Foundation. For in the absence of generally accepted graduate training programs for college and university administrators, the internship in the president's office seems to me one of the most promising means for training or finding good presidential material. Thus I would consider it not just desirable but virtually mandatory for the college president himself to assume the role of pedagogue in both seeking out and training young men and women with promising talent.

From reports from the ACE interns, it is quite obvious that the way the president uses his assistant is of vital importance. (I would remind you, Stanley, that the inspiration for these letters grew not only out of your inquiry but from the many hours of helpful discussions I have had with interns assigned to me under the ACE program.) The two biggest dangers are, first, that the president will be too busy to spend any time with his intern and, second, that he will not design a program in terms of the latter's interests and needs. At the very least the young aspirant should have an opportunity to read all the incoming and outgoing mail. He should be encouraged to attend as many committee meetings as possible and should sit with the president's cabinet. He should have an opportunity to spend periods of time in various other key administrative offices and should be given certain specific problems to bird-dog, analyze, and report. He should handle basic correspondence and even, if his talents lie in that direction, sketch out presidential addresses. He should be seen frequently in the presence of his chief, if possible on both social and professional occasions. And, finally, he should be able to attend regional and national meetings of administrators (particularly if he needs a job at the end of his internship!).

I have always considered myself fortunate in having had, in my early years, what could rightly be called an internship which extended over six years. During this period I had an opportunity to serve as liaison in almost every phase of university operation except the purely financial; and, perhaps most important of all, in preparing the first draft of the president's annual report I was obliged to see the relationship of the parts to the whole.

Perhaps a few gratuitous remarks to the prospective intern

might be in order here. Remember that the president is a busy, harried, and probably frustrated man. Don't demand any more of his time than can be used profitably by both of you, and never come back to him with a task only half completed. If you can, read some of his more recent speeches so that you can form an estimate of the man's administrative style. Behind the paneled walls of his office are many secrets. To the extent that he shares them with you, keep them to yourself. And perhaps most emphatically, stay strictly out of campus politics. People will be constantly brushing against you in hopes of finding out what the Old Man is thinking. Be his eyes and ears but pass on only that which in your most mature judgment is worthy of his attention. To extend this any further would be risking the same aftermath that accompanied Polonius' advice to Laertes!

As I vaguely recall, in an earlier letter I alluded to the practice of bringing one's own team along to a new setting. I know at least one outstanding university administrator for whom this has been a consistent policy, and certainly it has its advantages. I know another, however, who did the same but was never able to overcome the consequent feeling of distrust among both the faculty and administration. Presumably the basic difference was the quality of his team and the way in which he used them in the new setting. Although I have brought mine with me on at least one occasion, my preference is very strongly in favor of operating with the administrative cadre I inherit in the new position and then making such gradual changes as circumstances dictate. Quite frequently one or more of the top echelon will submit a "courtesy" resignation to the new president, a resignation which generally would be wisely ignored. For these individuals are likely to be the least insecure and ultimately the most loyal and effective.

Some administrators are vastly more successful than others in being able to remove members of their staff without hard feelings or, perhaps more importantly, without suffering immense personal anguish. I look at these individuals with envy. College and university administration, unlike that in business and industry, seems to me inevitably a much more personal thing. Moreover, the president generally does not have to appear before an annual stockholders' meeting and explain why the profits have been falling. As a result, we tend to tolerate inefficiency so long as the individual concerned has at least some redeeming features. When a move is inevitable we try him in some other spot before severing the umbilical cord altogether. One reason, perhaps, for this tolerance is the fact that his counterparts on the faculty have earned permanent tenure and thus are virtually unremovable except in extremis. Administrators, too, in many public systems, are beginning to earn permanent tenure; and there have actually been instances where a president has been taken to court by a member of his staff whom he has tried to remove. Fortunately, the courts to date have taken the attitude that this is the university's own business, but I have no predictions for the future.

To paraphrase Macbeth, "If it were done when 'tis done," then the best thing is to do it quickly. Generally we know within a year whether a man has the qualities the job requires. This means that each probationary administrator should have some kind of annual review in writing, which can be discussed with his immediate superior as well as with the individual himself. But it is grossly unfair to allow a situation to drag on—as I have allowed situations to drag on from time to time, mea culpa.

The most difficult problem, of course, is with the man who after years in the job is found incapable of matching its new dimensions. The first effort should be to provide additional staff, but this doesn't always turn the trick. Next we try to find him some other spot in the administration, but this can rarely be done without playing musical chairs. Finally, if the budget will allow, we create a new position with a new title and bring someone in over his head. You will notice that we have not fired him and that we are simply waiting for the day when he can be persuaded into early retirement.

Even in a fairly large university, I would strongly favor having the president interview at least briefly all of the top candidates for administrative positions down to the third or fourth or perhaps even the fifth level. In this way he inevitably shares a portion of the blame for mistakes in hiring. On the more positive side, by virtue of his position he is the best salesman for the institution and can often add that final note of persuasion necessary to obtain the best available man in today's very competitive market. The interview also can initiate the kind of relationship that will make the new man feel free to talk directly with the president, should this ever seem desirable. And incidentally, where a consultative committee is involved in recommending new administrators for the president's final approval (and this applies to the lower administrative levels as well), he should always insist on having at least three nominations presented to him. It does not particularly matter if the committee wishes to present these names in an order of preference, so long as it is clearly understood that the president will make the final choice.

As to the president's relationships with his staff, this is very much a matter of that administrative style I talked about in an earlier letter. I suppose it is inevitable that we tend to listen to certain of our associates more than to others. It is even possible that we listen more to the ones whom we recruited than to those we inherited.

The most successful administrator, I am convinced, is the one who has the knack of making every man on his staff feel important. This is quite different, of course, from making them feel happy. It is entirely up to them whether or not they achieve that other important life goal. The president, however, should never play obvious favorites, a rule which must apply in social as well as professional relationships with the members of the team. I would even suggest passing this caveat on to your wife, whose role in the matter of administrative relationships is by no means inconsequential. She should, for example, encourage you to have at least one relaxed social event annually in which you invite as many husbands and wives as possible from the administrative cadre. She should also learn to call all the wives by their first names, since you are not likely to have this opportunity or talent. Other than that, I am sure that she will need very little advice from the likes of me. (I hope you agree, Mary.)

One final note, touching upon something which I alluded to earlier—there is always a certain amount of jealousy over who will serve in the president's kitchen cabinet. If the organizational structure is clear enough and well differentiated, then the answer lies merely in limitation along lines of administrative echelons. Inevitably, though, you will be confronted with a very logical argument why such and such a person who operates outside of the delineated levels should be included. The moment an exception is made, you will quickly be confronted with requests for other very logical exceptions; and if you are not careful, the kitchen cabinet will look like the kitchen at the Waldorf. Obviously, no one should attend cabinet meetings regularly who is not concerned with most of the problems to be discussed. Others can be invited from time to time as consultants, resource persons, choose what rubric you will. I would urge, nevertheless, that you have periodic meetings with as wide a range of your administrative personnel as possible, preferably meetings that take place off campus, where the temptation to answer the telephone is reduced to a minimum.

I have never hesitated to hold administrative meetings during times when the academic staff may be on vacation; and if you want to make a real impression when you first assume the presidency, start holding regular meetings at seven or seven-thirty on Monday mornings, as did the incoming president some years ago at a major university where I was serving. The results in that previously rather sleepy organization were nothing short of spectacular. Since I left only a few months after the new regimen was instituted, I don't know at what point the dawn patrol may subsequently have been discontinued. I suspect the president had found out in advance that his predecessor never spent more than one or two hours a day in the office and that even those in the second and third echelons were inclined to arrive around ten in the morning and leave again by four-thirty in the afternoon at least during tennis weather.

For the sake of our personal relationship, Stanley, as well as to preserve some degree of domestic tranquillity, I shall bring this letter to a close and start out to test whether Michelin is wrong or right about the restaurants of Lyon.

As ever,

Le Président Malgré Lui

80

Dear Stanley:

I thought today I might visit the University of Paris at Nanterre, where last year's student revolution (which nearly unseated the government) is said to have begun. My better judgment prevailed, however; for I doubt very much that I could offer anything to solve their problems. It is even possible that the presence of an American college administrator might contribute somewhat to them. Consequently, while waiting for the Musée Rodin to open, I will try my hand at a few of the more or less random thoughts which Nanterre brought to mind.

I remember many years ago reading the results of a survey of college presidents in which they were asked to list their most besetting problems. One of the respondents reportedly replied, "I don't know any problems which I don't have." An exaggeration perhaps, but an exaggeration of an essential truth. For as I sat down a while ago to think of some of the problems, particularly with regard to personnel, which confront the president, I was nearly overwhelmed by the upsurge which flowed from thirty years of administrative recollection.

By a curious coincidence I found awaiting me at the American Express a packet of mail from the office, including a "Questionnaire Tally on Most Frustrating Problems of College and University Presidents," a survey conducted in 1968 by an organization known as the International Association of University Presidents. Since you can very likely get hold of this for yourself, I will simply list a few of the principal frustrations in order to get this letter underway. At the very top (261 out of 391) is, naturally enough, sky-

81

rocketing costs. Competing for second place are "inability of an institution to become as outstanding as he should like it to be" and "pressures of 'rat-race' schedule." Next in descending order are "unreasonable demands of students" and "unreasonable demands of professors," with 105 and 103 each. Then dropping down to the 60s are "inability to get outstanding students," "inefficiency of administrators," and "inability to get rid of unworthy faculty members." But before this dismal array discourages you too much, let me quickly add that 284 of the 391 college and university presidents seemed to be "having a wonderful time." Sic transit gloria statistici!

There can be little doubt that financial problems have always been and probably always will be skirting the insoluble in university administration, and the president cannot avoid being continuously perplexed by them. As the official campus dreamer, however, he cannot allow himself to be overwhelmed thereby. I have served in a few administrations where the budget was a deep dark secret whose full details were known only to the very top echelon. I even learned, in those days, a few useful tricks of budgetary legerdemain which I do not intend to share with you at this particular stage of your administrative development. I have, however, come to be a strong supporter of the open budget plan whereby anyone who wishes may have a "look-see." This tactical point of view is not without its hazards. No administrator can budget with complete success for the unforeseen, and it is only good business to provide for contingencies. I suspect, moreover, that the practice of concealing these reserves, or at least a portion of them, is just as common in colleges and universities as it is in business institutions. I remember an old pastor friend of mine pointing out how unwise it was for a nonprofit agency ever to be out of the red!

On the other hand, because the academic salary budget is inevitably the major item of expense, I think that the time is long overdue for the faculty to bear greater responsibility in trying to resolve the fiscal problems of our colleges and universities; but they can scarcely be expected to do this unless they also have a share in budget formulation. Thus, even though a faculty budget committee often is merely a kind of charade, it seems to me that the game is well worth the playing. Nor do I mean to sound even remotely cynical here. It is merely a fact that most faculty members are too busy with other responsibilities to willingly take the time required for a thorough understanding of the intricacies of academic budget making. How many of them, for example, would voluntarily read the two-volume book on college fiscal affairs prepared under the auspices of the American Council on Education and the National Association of College and University Business Officers? To be frank with you, I have not read all of it either. On the other hand, years ago I did read through a much simpler guidebook on college budget making and must say, with a proper degree of modesty, that I have also learned a bit from experience. You will merely ascribe it to human fallibility, I hope, when I confess with what satisfaction I once discovered that a financial officer, with whom I was having less than cordial relations, had made a small error of a million dollars in a long-range budget projection! To balance this off, I will have to confess that my budget one year fell short by one hundred and fifty thousand dollars because of an unexpected drop in enrollment. Fortunately, we had three contingency accounts (two of which were concealed) which more than covered the projected deficit.

I would urge that you make certain your budget procedures follow a national, standardized pattern. Although there is always room for local variation to meet peculiarities in the individual system, the benefit in being able to compare cost percentages is incalculable. For example, in one institution we discovered that our admissions costs were substantially below those of comparable colleges and universities. With this as a spur we were able to bring about much-needed improvements with a minimum of resistance. I would also insist on monthly or at least quarterly reports so that you can see at a glance which programs are living within their budget and which are not.

If I could begin my education over again, I would take one or two courses in accounting and a good solid course in statistics.

There is a rumor that the wave of the future in business and industry will see top management taken over by those who specialize in computer science. Although I would make no such prediction for colleges and universities—still being something of a romanticist— I think nevertheless that the president must at least have a working knowledge in these areas so that his decisions can profit from the kinds of information they generate. Unfortunately I have rarely known a decision that had the benefit of all possible information. This makes all the more important the president's ability to interpret such data as are available.

The ideal organizational setup, one which could minimize the president's problems, fiscal and otherwise, and maximize institutional effectiveness, would be to have a vice-president for planning who would be a free-wheeling staff and quasi-line officer. He would have access to every office and ultimate control over none. Among his functions would be the preparation and updating annually of a five- and a ten-year fiscal projection based on the long-range academic goals of the institution—goals which would be periodically reassessed by him and the president on three-day pack trips into the French Alps. Another of his functions would be continuous evaluation of any and every program in the institution. He would, of course, be in charge of the periodic self-studies required by the various accrediting bodies; but if he were really performing his role, these studies would be carried on continuously. He would also function as the administrative troubleshooter. As such he would be concerned with managerial efficiency in every administrative operation of the institution. One of his first tasks would certainly be to look over every form letter, in fact every form, used anywhere in the university. Which leads me to what I consider to be his final, but by no means least important, responsibility, and that is to ensure an efficient flow of information throughout the institution. To borrow a naval term, he would be in effect the chief communications officer, a role of significant proportions. And on at least one day a week he would be paid time and a half merely to sit with his feet propped up on his desk, a desk cleared of everything except a snapshot of his wife and kiddies at their summer home at the shore. The absence of such an officer is one of the most inexcusable and false economies in all of higher education.

And now I am off to the Musée.

Au revoir,

Charles

Dear Stanley:

In my last letter, in thinking over the range of problems that beset the president, I did not get very far beyond fiscal concerns. I recognize that at the most I revealed a few prejudices of my own and provided nothing in the way of lasting solutions. An old friend of mine, a college president who died a few years ago, used to begin his talks to various alumni groups with, "We have no problems at dear old Backwash which a few million dollars couldn't solve." That may have been good for a fund-raising pitch but it certainly was an oversimplification.

As much as I would like to, I suppose I cannot skip altogether the question of fund raising; for the president, whether of a private or tax-supported institution, cannot avoid this harassing preoccupation. In fact, many presidents are elected to office because of demonstrated talents in whacking the bushes. Since I do not consider that my own talents have been unusual in this department, the following observations may appear to be singularly unromantic. At least they are brief.

Brevity is not inappropriate here; for the written material on the subject of institutional fund raising is as ubiquitous as are the chestnut trees along the Champs Élysées. Nearly all of the leading development consulting firms, in fact, seem to publish brochures and newsletters telling how gold is to be prospected. They all imply, of course, that the first approach is to engage their services. Unfortunately, they are right, which doesn't mean that any particular one is the right one for you. Like choosing a wife or a vice-president, the successful selection of a consulting firm is often a matter of luck. My best advice is to ease in by investing in a preliminary probability study. If they tell you that you have the best prospects for a successful fund-raising program of any college in the country, don't touch them with a ten-foot mace. Nevertheless, this preliminary study, at a cost of five to ten thousand dollars, is probably unavoidable.

Finding an effective consultant firm is not half so difficult, however, as finding a good director of development. You will notice, Stanley, that I accept the hypothesis that both are necessary. The former is often very useful in finding the latter. At any rate, the preliminary study, whether the president likes it or not, very likely gives him and the members of his board a fairly good idea as to the type of development program that is feasible and therefore the type of man who is needed. I personally have a sheer horror of campaigns, while recognizing that very often they are dictated by the situation. Participation in an effort to meet a Ford Challenge Grant some years ago has left me in a state that best can be described as gun-shy. My impression from having recruited directors of development is that there are ten "campaign" types to one "development" officer. The explanation, of course, lies in the fact that multimillion dollar campaigns by large universities do in fact come to a close now and again, thereby dumping on the market a lot of high-pressure talent. That it is usually also fairly high-priced talent goes without saying. But here, as in public relations, there is so much competition for the really first-rate individual that the sky seems almost the limit. Occasionally a man is willing to leave one of the consulting firms in order to run his own show. I need hardly point out, though, that there is a basic psychological difference between being a consultant and being the director of a long-range fund-raising effort. Thus, a better source of personnel is often the second echelon in a large university development program. I don't discount either the effectiveness of running ads in the appropriate journals, but this makes the screening job all the more hazardous.

In the long run the success or failure of any fund-raising effort lies with the president. Perhaps this is the only area where he really is essential. On the other hand, it is not every president's cup of tea. I knew one man quite well who was endowed with unusual social charms and many wealthy friends; but by temperament he found it excruciatingly difficult to ask any of the latter for a cent, so difficult that his health actually suffered when the time occurred in his university's fiscal condition that fund-raising was no longer avoidable.

Since, as I said, this is an area of presidential responsibility on which there is a vast amount of literature available, it would certainly seem redundant to spend more time here, except to say that unless the president has the proper temperament and unless the trustees are willing to make personal contributions of both time and money, he had better think very carefully before committing his precious energies to this effort.

Finally, I would repeat my personal predilection against campaigns. The term "development" is not just a euphemism. The process is slow and arduous. One of the major West Coast universities that has been notably successful in fund raising never asks a prospect for a contribution until he has been cultivated for at least three years. Furthermore, despite the president's focal role, a long-range program is usually successful only if there is wide faculty participation as well—though there is a general reluctance on the part of the teaching staff to be concerned with anything so sordid as money. The president of an outstanding private college in the Midwest told me recently that contacts forged by members of the faculty brought in millions of dollars in five years. The president and the appropriate members of his staff and faculty should, of course, cooperate in cultivating foundation sources, but I would caution you that these are far less lucrative wellsprings of support than many trustees would like to think. The new tax laws may limit this source even more. Finally, fund raising, like charity, really must begin at home—with the trustees, with alumni, with the local community. Unless support is available from those who presumably know the institution best, it is not likely to descend like manna from the distant skies.

If you knew my own experiences in this sensitive activity, Stanley, I could appropriately close this letter with "quod erat demonstrandum." But here in our hotel room in Paris it all seems just a little remote.

Adieu,

Charles

88

Dear Stanley:

When I studied formal logic many long years ago I was assured by my professor that the classical dilemma exists very rarely in nature. I must advise you, Stanley, that the nature of the president's calling skews the figures dangerously. As I sit here in Le Bois de Boulogne, mentally reviewing many checkered careers, it seems that the president no more survives one classical dilemma than he is caught in another. Nor can he normally detect them as they edge over the horizon. When they move into view they are usually, like Venus on the half shell, fully blown.

The college president seems continuously to be confronted with "uptight" situations where he must reach a rapid decision, in the full knowledge that any decision is bound to be wrong. This is his classical dilemma. It is varied only by situations where he may have a choice of three decisions, any one of which is wrong. A classical trilemma!

The conscientious president—and who among us is not—will first ascertain all the available facts. Since the most important facts are often not knowable, this means that he inevitably has far less information than he should have for his internal computer mechanism to operate effectively. Next, or more likely simultaneously, and assuming that there is time, he must consult with everyone available, including (1) all those who will be affected by his decision, (2) the forunate few who will not be affected, (3) the official consultative committee or committees, (4) his administrative family, (5) his secretary, (6) his wife, and (7) in the tradition of Gilbert and Sullivan, his uncles, his cousins, and his aunts.

Following this rigorous (and time-consuming) survey, he will normally devote a minimum of three sleepless nights, punctuated by frantic but fruitless efforts to find a rationale for postponing or avoiding the decision altogether. But finally, as happens to all dies, the die must be cast, the decision made.

At this point I have a very earnest recommendation, which is for the president to get out of town for an extended period, preferably on a critical mission that had been scheduled many months in advance. Otherwise, under proper medical advice, he might undertake a moderate regimen of equanol, warm baths, and so forth.

These remarks are by no means to be taken as frivolous. As justification, I offer a not untypical example which occurred on a sylvan campus to be known temporarily as "X." Among other things, I believe this example proves the old saw that "a little college is a dangerous thing." It also demonstrates that the president is not unlike John Erskine's small boy walking atop a picket fence. That the experience is thrilling makes it nonetheless hazardous.

The trustees of X, responding to local faculty pressure and the national policies of, among others, the AAUP, had a long-established principle that in personnel matters the president should accept the recommendations of the appropriate faculty consultative bodies. If he feels there are compelling reasons why he cannot, the burden of proof is on him and, what's more, he is expected to state his reasons in writing. His greatest hope, in extremis, is that he will be subject neither to charges of libel nor AAUP blacklisting—fates only slightly less unacceptable than a hasty demise.

Within this comfortable frame of reference, our president discovered on a melancholy Tuesday morning that a department, after full consultation with its members, both faculty and student, had committed a teaching position (even though it did not possess such authority) to a highly controversial and even dubiously qualified instructor. As is not unusual, the president first learned of the situation through the news media, which meant that the trustees and the local veterans' associations, not to mention the ACLU, were equally well informed, as were the opposing factions among his faculty. The fat was in the fire.

90

Despite his most earnest efforts to dissuade the department from pressing its nomination, they assured him that their candidate was the best available under the college's poor competitive position and in view of the highly specialized academic need which only this individual could fill and only the department could understand. As the controversy thickened, in fact, the candidate in question automatically gained in academic distinction and desirability. Unfortunately, the trustees were unenlightened. In emergency session, the board quickly assumed the adamant position that the man was under no circumstances to be allowed in the classroom where he could despoil the pure minds of the students, male and female. The president's explanation to the effect that changing conditions in today's revolutionary climate may call for more flexible requirements at best inspired a few sotto voce observations about weak-kneed administrators.

In the meantime two other developments are worth noting. The local faculty association, whose active membership had been declining for several years in direct proportion to generous annual increases in salaries and fringe benefits, at long last had some foolproof issues—the integrity of faculty decision-making power, departmental autonomy, academic freedom, trustee infringement, you name it. Old placards were dusted off and shared with the campus chapter of Students for Responsible Anarchy. Since reaction breeds counteraction, the newly formed Students for Resistance to Student-Faculty Anarchy scheduled all-night strategy sessions with guidance from faculty advisers. Thus a number of irresistible forces were now confronting a number of immovable objects.

But there is one character we must not lose sight of. I refer to the small, lonely, Chaplinesque figure of the president. He knew that the secret of administrative success in such contretemps is to prevent the enemy from becoming either heroes or martyrs. He did not know with equal clarity, however, who was the enemy.

One of his options was to tender his resignation, thus adding at least ten years to his life. But presidents are not hired to resign—only to be removed from office. Further, this would be passing the buck, and as a dedicated administrator he believed in the principles

91

FREDERIC W. NESS

of responsibility and accountability. Any time, through his absten-
tion, a decision is engineered at a higher level he weakens his own
sense of integrity and contributes to the unfortunately widespread
belief that campus difficulties are to be blamed on the "fact" that
top administration fears to act decisively.

Is there a denouement, Stanley, to this tragicomedy? Yes,
but, like the epitaph of a notable potentate, the agonies may become immersed in universal laughter. You surely remember this
epitaph:

> Here lies our Sovereign Lord, the King,
> Whose word no man relies on.
> He never said a foolish thing,
> Nor ever did a wise one.

Eschewing all feminine endings (if I remember my art of poesy
accurately), I will adapt this to close today's rather disheartening
epistle (blame it on cloudy skies and some bad vin de maison):

> Here sits our unlamented President,
> With furrowed brow and heavy heart.
> He knows he's but a short-lived resident,
> But doesn't know quite when the putsch will start.

With apologies,

C. J.

P.S.   Oh yes, our president actually survived this episode—only
because campus and trustee attention were diverted by a more serious crisis.

$\mathcal{D}$ear $\mathcal{M}$ary:

Here we are leaving the sunshine of France and moving into the ubiquitous showers of the south coast of England. This climate may be wonderful for complexions, but what it can do for dispositions! Little wonder that the greatest humorists in the English language come from Ireland and not from the shores of Merry(?) England. But is the Irish climate any better? Little wonder, too, that Marjorie, whose disposition is second to none, has just reminded me somewhat testily that I have as yet written nothing to you in your role as a prospective dean's or president's wife. My obvious retort was that she, after all, is the logical one to write such a letter; but this was met with what could only be described as a stony silence. So here goes.

If you have read any of my notes to "Dear Stanley" (and I rather hope you didn't) you would have come across bits and snippets about your future role. Don't be disheartened by any of them, however, for the activities of the prexie's mate are just about as varied as she wishes them to be. At the annual meetings of the Association of American Colleges the wives periodically have a scheduled session for mutual interchange and consolation, and here's the place you can get the real lowdown. In particular you can find out what you don't want to be or do; but meantime here are a few animadversions of my own—pretty much as they happen to occur to me.

In the first place, talk the whole thing over with Stanley before you let him make the decision to become even a dean, let alone a president. I have personally known both a dean's wife and

93

a president's wife who were simply not suited by temperament for the role, and neither they nor their husbands had a very easy time of it. In one rather pathetic instance the wife of a dean-elect accompanied her spouse to the new campus, helped him buy a house, chose the draperies, and so on. When the time came to make the move, she refused to go along; and while obviously there must have been other domestic differences involved, the agonies went well beyond the immediate household. I once inherited, in a college home, a lovely dining-room set, with a particularly interesting table. According to legend, the president and his wife dined together, with him at one end and her at the other. As their relations began to deteriorate under the strains of the job, the loving pair increased the distance between them by adding leaves to the table. When the final one was put in place and the table could be expanded no farther, she reportedly packed her bags and left the gentleman to his own devices.

Divorce is bad enough under the best of circumstances, but even in today's rather permissive campus climate, divorce at this level is particularly painful; for, unfortunately, the dean and president, as well as their wives, are quasi-public property. Or to express this another way, they are always "good" news. Their comings and goings are of interest to the curious—and who among us is not curious!

At any rate, one of the most difficult adjustments for any president's wife is to the realization that she is constantly being watched. What she says, what she wears, what she does are immediate grist for the gossip mills, and the smaller the campus the gristier the mill. The only wife whose visibility is probably greater is the wife of a minister or an ambassador, but 'twas ever thus!

Partly for this reason I would urge you, if you have a choice, never to live on campus. Living on campus is little different from pitching a tent in Grand Central Station. Even in this day of washers and driers, there are times when, perhaps only out of nostalgia, you might wish to hang something out on a line. But, believe me, you will hesitate long before doing so. After all, who wants even his clean linen displayed to public view? And when you feel moved to sit in the sun, clad only in your bikini, you will immediately be aware of all those Sigma Chis finding a need to shortcut through your backyard. Even when Dick and Jane and Spot—I refer to your little darlings and their four-legged companion—release their youthful spirits you will nervously wish they had a few more inhibitions. Pure imagination on my part? Well, I recall when my then five-year-old, armed with two cap pistols, jumped from behind a bush and challenged a stuffy, aging professor of economics. The good gentleman has not forgiven me to this day!

Otherwise, living on campus was a great experience for my children. One (female) became an honorary member of one of the fraternities. Another always had expert help with his homework, after he discovered that I was less than useless as a source of aid. Let me add only that they all grew up a little more rapidly than either Marjorie or I might have wished.

But let's assume that you have no choice except to live in the traditional president's home—which could be anything from a half-million-dollar mansion to a hundred-year-old house given to the institution by the local coal dealer whose mate threatened to go home to mother if he didn't get them away from the encroaching undergraduates. One such president's home which I visited frequently had been built in two stages. Every time there was a change in temperature the edifice cracked and creaked like something in a grade-B horror movie.

There is the positive side to all this, however. The college-provided house is worth at least five thousand dollars a year in salary, a sum not readily made up by a living allowance for those who would seek their own accommodation. Further, it is infinitely comforting these days just to be able to call the plant department when a pipe springs a leak.

I vividly recall, though, one college home I lived in where our neighbors were a fraternity house on one side—a fraternity which was affectionately known throughout the campus as "the animal farm"—and the college gym on the other. As if this were not bad enough, the house fronted on a main street which was also a national highway. Often during the night cattle trucks would stop

95

in front of us while the driver, with an electric prod, stirred his cargo into a state of wakefulness so that they would not be tempted to lie down. As a confirmed insomniac, I will refrain from telling you what I was frequently goaded into doing! But enough of this.

You may one day be faced with the interesting experience of being offered a new presidential manse, a heady experience at best. If this occurs, I can assure you that it will involve a real test of someone's character—perhaps yours. It happened to us in an almost classical manner. A member of the board of trustees and his lovely wife, cognizant of certain shortcomings in the old president's home, and expecting to retire to an area appropriate to a more relaxed way of life, wished to offer us their twenty-two-room home, swimming pool, orange grove, et al. They did not, however, approach us directly, fearing that we might feel obliged to accept the offer. Instead they asked two of our mutual friends to take us to dinner for the purpose of sounding us out first. Such sensitivity, I assure you, is a rare and wonderful quality!

We were, of course, both delighted and eager. Soon thereafter the word began to leak out. In a matter of days, and before the negotiations had come far along, I received a very thoughtful letter from an old friend, a man who had long been a kind of mentor to me, urging us not to accept and giving no less than fourteen reasons to support his advice. Among them was the quite convincing argument that the very elegance of the establishment was likely to create envy among others in the university family and even among many of the alumni. Further, he pointed out, the degree of privacy which we had enjoyed in the other house would be lost to us as various individuals and organizations would seek to utilize the house or grounds for a variety of activities. The cost of maintenance would also be a problem, one that would certainly not escape the attention of potential donors, not to mention taxpayers. What is more, he illustrated the point by reminding me of several other presidents, two of whom I knew about, who had come to grief over building or accepting houses that were clearly in the extravagance range. One of these situations resulted in a hassle that made the pages of newspapers from coast to coast and nearly resulted in a forced resignation.

With such stern and wise advice you might have expected me to make an equally wise decision and turn down the offer. If so, you underestimate my capacity for rationalization! Because only three of the other presidents in our large state system had homes provided them we were persuaded that the publicity which was likely to be given to our acquisition might encourage other boards to seek houses for their presidents. But this was the lesser of the two determinative rationalizations. The other was more subtle and even more speculative. Our college had for many years been a normal school. Shortly after it began to grow in scope it developed an excellent agricultural department. And regardless of the fact that it had advanced far beyond those two interests, its reputation in its support area was still that of a normal school which also taught agriculture to those who couldn't go to the university, a hundred or so miles away. In short, the college enjoyed little or no social status. When potential donors felt a mood of generosity coming over them, they instinctively thought of the university or of one of the better known private colleges in the state.

Well, let me say merely that during our years in the new president's home these attitudes changed substantially and that the house itself had something to do with the transformation. Furthermore, immediately on our moving in, the board passed a resolution to the effect that the president's house was his home and that the only entertaining to be carried on therein should be entertaining which he or his wife elected to initiate or sponsor. The wisdom of this action was immediately apparent to us, for within a matter of days we had a half dozen inquiries from groups, several of which had not the slightest connection with the college, wishing to use our home for their meetings or social events. The fact is, we did do a great deal of entertaining, but only because we happen both to be gregarious characters and love no parties better than our own. As Marj once described one of her soirées to me, she had merely invited "three or four hundred of her most intimate friends!"

Now another caution. Don't be persuaded, even by the longest and most sacred of institutional traditions, to let yourself run a campus hotel. I knew well one college where the president had been expected for decades to provide hospitality for the chairman of the board on his all too frequent visits to town, as well as for any and all "distinguished" visitors, of whom there was a never-ending procession. The president's wife, who was a little jaundiced about her role anyway, became a positive hypochondriac and managed to spend most of each academic year in their summer retreat in a warmer clime.

So get a few things squared away before you ever let Stanley say yes. Among other things, be sure that you demand adequate household help as one of the perquisites of the job. No matter how tight the college budget may be—and always is—you are an integral part of the president's job and have as much a right to one or two full-time helpers as he does to his secretarial staff. You will be surprised to discover how easy it is to get a full-time gardener on the college budget, but how difficult it often is to get adequate provision for household help.

In one of my letters to Stanley I commented on administrative style. The style of the president's wife can be equally important. To my list of don'ts, therefore, let me add another. Don't try to be like the previous president's wife. You will undoubtedly hear remarks to the effect, "Mrs. ——— did so and so." Fine, that was her style. It doesn't have to be yours. In all probability you couldn't do it her way even if you wanted to. Just don't try. Be yourself.

This applies even to your dress, though here a few words of caution may be in order. Despite the relaxation which has been evident in recent years, I don't think that many deans' or presidents' wives even now would appear at a faculty party in décolleté. Go ahead and try it if the spirit moves, but remember that faculty wives in general are living on a more limited budget—a fact which should not be made too obvious by your *haute couture*. (Some of them, of course, can afford to outshine you under any circumstances, but then "Who's Afraid of Virginia Woolf?") I knew one dean's wife who not only had campus social responsibilities but also ran an art gallery in a nearby city. This poor lady had to sport two quite separate wardrobes, alas and alack!

Need I say that although the college president's wife has been described as an unpaid presidential assistant, she is likely to raise eyebrows if she casts herself in the role of a college officer. It is a mistake, for instance, for her to demand any special privileges on campus or to make more than the most sparing personal use of college property, such as an official car—let alone to let herself get mixed up in campus politics.

Now on the subject of entertainment. You are still presumably too young to know whether you like big "do's" or not; but as a president's wife you will be called on for the most varied sorts of hostessing. Many presidential teams believe in frequent and elaborate entertaining of students, and this can serve a very useful purpose. I was acquainted with one wife who abruptly gave it up when an undergraduate guest wrote an editorial in the campus paper which was something less than gracious about a particular student buffet over which the good lady had expended much thought and energy. Nor can she be blamed. Among other things, the student complained about what she considered the unattractive china used on the table. Presumably nothing short of Spode for sixty would have turned the trick. Further, not one student was gracious enough to write a thank-you note.

I have known several other wives who always held high tea on Sunday afternoons for any students or faculty who wished to drop in; and these were pleasurable occasions for the guests. But basically, my sage advice would be to remember that yours is a home, not a house, and that your first obligations are to your own family.

There are all sorts of other odds and ends I could tuck in here, mostly from the secondhand observation of that superbly skilled hostess whom I was lucky enough to have spoused (I still think she should be writing this letter). For example, don't follow the practice of another president's wife who, whenever she entertained a largish faculty group, drafted faculty wives as kitchen help. If you can't do it any other way, don't do it. If you wish to let the faculty wives use your house for a party, don't you be the hostess. And don't be so involved in the details of a party that you are not yourself on hand to greet and talk with the guests. After all, you probably know the names of the faculty wives much better than your husband, who therefore needs you by his side.

And remember your responsibility to protect both the family silver and the family budget. One year we discovered, in the absence of an adequate expense account, that we had used well over a thousand of our own hard-earned dollars in official entertaining. The fact that you can take some of this off your income tax does not provide adequate justification. Stanley, of course, will always be worried about shortages in the college budget. It is your job to see that he is equally concerned with the family budget, even though he will probably turn its management over to you.

To revert for a moment to the subject of students and faculty, let me caution you against becoming a mother hen. Because I know you well, I see little real danger. And yet it is an almost irresistible urge—an urge which, of course, at times should not be resisted. I remember early in my (I mean "our") administrative career when, on a tip from a housemother, Marjorie and I went to the women's dormitory together and brought a student home with us. After an hour or so of motherly counsel, Marjorie persuaded her to let us take her to the hospital. Unfortunately, it was too late. Three days later she died of uremic poisoning. On the larger campus, of course, these problems rarely reach the president or his wife, but even here it is surprising how tenaciously the principle of *in loco parentis* seems to cling.

As for the faculty, you may remember my cautioning Stanley against becoming too intimate with any particular faculty members, referring to the loss of friendship as a price one pays for accepting the office. This is equally applicable to you, unfortunately. The greatest difficulty occurs when you move up within your own institution, for in this circumstance your social ties with certain faculty wives will have already been formed. Decisions made in his office, campus political polarizations, even understandable jealousy over his own preferment may affect these long-standing relationships;

100

and you will simply have to be mature enough to realize that this too will pass.

Like a physician's wife, you must not become a source of information. You cannot, of course, if Stanley tells you nothing. But since, as I implied in an earlier letter, he has few other people in whom he can afford to confide, in the loneliness of his position he has a right to tell you, and you have an obligation to listen and to tell no one. A Spartan admonition!

Finally—though now that I am nearly finished with this letter and the Dover docks are in clear but rainy view Marjorie will doubtless think of many things which I should have said—let me comment briefly on the faculty wives' club (at one college, affectionately referred to as "The Campus Followers"). After having participated in the founding of one such organized gaggle, Marjorie is convinced that the president's or dean's wife should not become, let alone remain, a prime mover. She attends when she wishes, makes our home available for one or more meetings a year, but refuses to accept any office or, for that matter, even to make any formal talks to the faculty wives. This is simply her personal "style." Her predecessor served as chairman of the club for years, made some kind of oration at most meetings, and had a gold star for perfect attendance. You take your choice.

But if you choose to become a dean's or a president's wife these are some of the joys you can anticipate. I am told, though, that it is also rather fun to be prima inter pares!

And here is Dover and our

warm affection,

Charles (and, by proxy, Marjorie)

ᐩ⬚═══⬚═══⬚═══⬚═══⬚═══⬚

Dear Mary:

I have just read Charles' letter, and since I refuse to be a postscript to my tender loving husband, I am enclosing my second thoughts to his first ones.

No matter how much you read or think about the years ahead, you can never fully anticipate the duties and concerns of the president's wife. As a matter of fact, you may find that you have not had much contact with that segment of the academic world and so are necessarily pretty unaware of what it entails. For example, when Charles accepted his first presidency, my only encounters with presidents' wives had been as a student at the university, seeing Mrs. Jones pouring tea or riding about town in a sleek limousine, behind a chauffeur. That seemed like a very happy prospect for me, soon shattered when we took up residence on our own campus and found out what life was really like in less opulent surroundings. Since then I have poured buckets of tea, but I'll never see the Cadillac and the driver!

And, too, how can I begin to tell you about the loneliness of the job??? I am neither fish nor fowl (faculty nor administration). I find myself walking alone; often, I suspect, I hear more of the criticism voiced by the local populace than Charles, for I am the one who grocery shops and trudges down Main Street.

Let me merely say that if you find yourself in the position and cannot get out, unless by death or divorce, (1) Keep your sense of humor, or develop one in a hurry; (2) Don't take yourself or your position too seriously, and try to remain natural and reasonably unassuming; (3) Above all, don't "wear the pants" for the family;

102

for I have witnessed wives ruining their husbands' careers by such a misguided change in role; (4) Walk in the middle of the line for everything, as for example, in clothing: choose between the extremes of Sears and Suzette's; (5) Make your own traditions, but keep them simple; (6) And finally, be prepared to pick up the pieces, with love of husband, children, and college.

I suppose I would do some things differently if we were starting over; but now that the end is in sight, I have no regrets, only friendly warnings to others. The compensations balance the heartaches, and I am still in one piece. Good luck!

Affectionately,

Marj

Dear Stanley:

The headlines in the London papers this morning were agog with the latest boudoir scandal. Who knows, on lesser issues governments have fallen! England and the United States may indeed be two nations divided by a common language, but in this instance one scarcely needs much familiarity with local patois to follow the seamy details.

All of which reminds me that I am arriving at an age where I am just a little startled at the freedom and total candor of the younger generation in its attitude toward sex. At the same time I rather envy their seeming lack of "hangup" with the subject. They appear to be avoiding some of the tensions and frustrations that so sorely afflicted my generation.

Although I perforce approach the subject here with the modesty appropriate to my condition in life, I must acknowledge that the dean and the president cannot avoid sex, even though, in some misguided way, they may wish to do so. Presumably referring to the dean of women, countless undergraduate "humor" magazines over the centuries have run the headline, "President and Dean to Stop Necking on Campus." With minor changes in terminology, it will probably continue into the invisible future. Moreover, if an academic year goes by without seeing sex rear its head in scandalous fashion, the fact must surely deserve special mention in the institutional annals.

One of the more uncomfortable possibilities for a dean or president is to return in a disciplinary role to the campus where he had passed his carefree and libidinous undergraduate years. When

104

a hapless culprit is brought before him, he is unusual indeed if his first impulse is not to point out to the lad where he made his blunder and how with only a little research he can get away with it next time—if he survives for another time.

We are moving into an era where the traditional *in loco parentis* concept is being phased out; but unfortunately the general public is still not fully alerted to the fact. I have always been amazed at how the most permissive of parents turn savagely critical of what they consider the inexcusable permissiveness of the college administration. The degree of their failure to control Junior is in direct ratio to their expectations from the college. It is through such cultural gaps that deans and presidents can easily fall to their destruction.

The English papers a few weeks back brandished public outrage over the alleged advocacy, by a university dean, of unmarried students dorming together. Even though in subsequent discussion with the vice-chancellor I learned that the remark had been untimely ripped out of context, the good gentleman, as the result of external pressures, was put out to pasture where he could commit no further outrage against public sensibilities. Yet as I sat having tea in a dormitory room at the same university with a young lady and her swain of the moment, she told me with mingled amusement and annoyance that, in the face of more adult policies in some other English universities, this particular one required male guests to leave the girls' rooms by midnight. "But," said she, "you should be around here some night when there is a three A.M. fire drill!"

This illustrates what is perhaps the worst aspect of sex on the campus—the enforced hypocrisy with which it has been treated at all but the more enlightened colleges. We have, to be sure, come a long way from my own undergraduate days when the dean of women had a rule that if a young lady found it necessary to sit on a gentleman's lap in a horseless carriage, she should place between them a copy of the Sunday *New York Times*. Quelle delicatesse!

Those were the days, too, when the pregnant coed was required on discovery to withdraw from college. There was decidedly a sexual double standard. The young man, even if identified, could

105

continue his studies none the worse for wear. Those were, in short, the innocent days B.P.—"before the pill."

In my earlier administrative years, as a functionary in the system, I participated in disciplinary extreme unction which today would be duplicated in only the most reactionary institutions—decisions for which I wish I could personally apologize to a half dozen individuals, even though they may well have gone on to become leading citizens. In fact, I should not be surprised to find them among the most straight-laced in their communities, for such are life's little ironies. Mercifully, however, I have forgotten their names, including even that of the young lady who, during a lean period, tried to work her way through college by practicing the oldest profession. No *New York Times* for her!

I would not have you think, Stanley, that I am in accord with the total license now practiced on some campuses. For example, I do not really approve of all-night visiting hours—but not out of moral compunction. Morality, I have noticed, scarcely operates by the clock. Principally I object because it usually entails an invasion of privacy. When one of my suite mates in college had his fiancée with him for two weeks the rest of us found the situation an unconscionable bore. I often meant to ask him if he didn't find it a bit tiresome himself.

The new mode, fascinating as it is, sorely tests the credulity of one of my generation. Although few colleges yet condone unmarried students living together in the dormitory, many now accept all-night visits in response to the students' insistence that the new sexual equality, the dimensions of friendship, and even the requirements of study make such visits essential. That intercourse occurs is a recognized fact; but there is little evidence to suggest that an easing of dormitory regulations is a significant factor in its frequency. In the search for even greater freedom, as you know, many students live off campus in a variety of convenient and some inconvenient combinations. But since you, Stanley, are closer to this way of life than I—I allude solely to our difference in years—let me merely observe that the dean and president are obliged to take cognizance of these arrangements with far less frequency today than would have been true even a decade ago. The mores of the campus community are such that there is little they could do about it even if they wanted to.

I would draw the line, however, where a member of the faculty seeks to preserve his youth by cavorting in gay abandon with the undergraduates, of whichever sex. Under most circumstances there should be some distance maintained between student and professor (as well as between student and administration). If each considers the other in every sense his equal, then the student should pay no fees and the professor should draw no salary.

Particularly reprehensible is the instructor who uses his position to take advantage of a student. I recall one situation when the best advice I could give a harassed coed was to be sure she always kept the desk between her and the professor. Complete peace was restored only when he retired. Another man I knew used to shock the maidens in his class by asking each one to provide a sample of her pubic hair. He of course protested that his interests were purely scientific (which at his age might indeed have been true), but there must have been a better way to pursue such a preoccupation. On another memorable occasion I was visited in my sanctuary by an irate mother, her hysterical daughter, and the family lawyer—in a real live Svengali case. Although the instructor insisted that, acting with the consent of the parents, he was applying hypnotism only to relieve the young lady of certain psychological difficulties, the circumstances were highly questionable. One or the other, if not both, was pretty naive. Fortunately (1) the family was ultimately persuaded that a court suit would not contribute to the young lady's peace of mind, such as she had; (2) I was reasonably persuaded that nothing had in fact happened, thanks possibly to a premature knock on the door; and (3) the faculty member was persuaded to accept early retirement in order to devote his talents to the private practice of hypnotherapy.

I have known of faculty members demanding that the president dismiss other faculty members because of alleged immorality, in several instances involving other faculty members' wives. I have known of similar demands from parents even after the instructor in

107

question had agreed to make an honest woman of their daughter in the presence of a parson. I have listened to frantic wives demanding that we force their philandering husbands to toe the straight and narrow. In all such cases the administrator has a deep and humane obligation—to be a sympathetic listener. He may even provide some stern counsel to the errant mate. But for him to go much farther in this day and age is to court disaster—not infrequently in a court of law. He can no more be father confessor to the staff than to the students.

In one irrational case, a friend of mine was relieved of his administrative responsibilities for allegedly having accused the entire freshman English staff of assigning their classes provocative reading materials in an effort to seduce the coeds. As one of his sympathetic fellow deans observed, the accusation was absurd on the face of it; for, as anyone in this business knows, it is not the instructor who tries to seduce the coed, but the other way around! On another occasion, a young teaching assistant reported to me that a student included with her final examination paper the key to her apartment and a note saying that she simply *had* to pass the course. Conscientious lad that he was, he gave her a well-deserved F. I subsequently ascertained that her semester's grades consisted of four F's and one A, from which I drew absolutely no conclusions.

The greatest difficulty in nearly every case involving sexual indiscretion is arriving anywhere near the truth. An academic community is supposed to be devoted to the pursuit of the truth, which merely proves how elusive a quarry the truth can be. When a situation becomes sticky some students will report confidentially and quite accurately on the behavior of a faculty member, particularly if a fellow student may be in danger of extreme discipline, but they will rarely provide testimony or evidence usable in a disciplinary hearing. Faculty members are not much different. They may (and often do) demand that the administration take action against one of their members, but they themselves will testify under only the direst circumstances.

Recently the social attitude toward the homosexual has been

108

undergoing change. For many years, however, homosexuality provided some of the most traumatic disciplinary problems with which the dean or president had to contend. It may well continue to do so for some years, the "gay liberation" movement notwithstanding. Regardless of the permissiveness in many of our social groups, the campus will usually be responsive to the median mores of its constituency. At the very least, therefore, the college has a right to expect members of its inner community to act with some degree of discretion and respect for the sensibilities of others. I say, with no great air of discovery, that academicians are just as human as other people. There are relatively few saints on the instructional budget.

The profession itself has not as yet faced squarely its own responsibilities. Under the fragile mantle of academic freedom it has blinked at abuses which have pushed academic freedom perilously close to destruction.

You may well ask, Stanley, how this last observation relates to the general substance of this letter—which I was inspired to address as the result both of the morning news and of a leisurely stroll through Soho earlier this evening. Well, perhaps it doesn't. Except that not long ago I had to defend before a legislative investigating committee—and I did so with a certain degree of brilliance—an art exhibit depicting some dozen or so very ingenious sexual positions, including a few of the more standard ones. At about the same time, in a campus debate on academic freedom, I listened to an "enlightened" departmental chairman declare that if B.R. (a leading philosopher of our day) were to put on a blatant sexual performance in the very midst of a student assembly this would, in his opinion, have no bearing upon the gentleman's acceptability as a member of our academic community.

The art exhibit I could conscientiously defend, particularly since I satisfied myself that this particular student (as well as his rather naive faculty mentor) was honestly striving for artistic expression and not setting out deliberately to challenge public sensibilities. Admittedly his artistic skill did not match his artistic integrity; but then, he is still young enough to develop the one and

109

degrade the other! But the assertion of the departmental chairman, though received enthusiastically by his particular student audience, I find wholly immature and unacceptable.

If this be a sign of my age, let me add only that I am glad I lived when I did.

Yours, de senectute,

Charles

P.S. The legislative investigation of our famous art exhibit had two interesting sidelights. The chairman of the committee admonished the witnesses on three occasions during the afternoon-long hearing that everything said there was strictly confidential. A public statement, if one were called for, would be made by him alone. When I arrived home several hours later from the state capitol my PR man called to ask me if I knew that there had been a line open throughout the testimony from the committee room directly to the press room. A detailed account of everything that had been said was being carried in and over all the media; and since I had made a vigorous, albeit extemporaneous, defense of freedom of artistic expression, my Neilson rating among the faculty liberals jumped to a short-lived and all-time high. What didn't get on the hot line was a conversation I had immediately after the hearing with one of the legislators who had given us a rather rough time. "It's not that we ourselves mind," he assured me sotto voce, "but, after all, we do have our constituency to think about." I have often wondered what careless aide left open that line to the press room!

110

Dear Stanley:

Yesterday's (or was it the day before?) meditation was inspired by the breaking of a scandal to an avid reading public. The British press, by comparison with the French and Italian, appears to exercise a highly commendable degree of reserve, especially in dealing with cases which are likely to go to the courts. I understand that they have developed this restraint the hard way. At times it seems to me that the only press in the world which exercises total freedom—perhaps license is the better term—is that which purports to speak for the students on the American campus. I make this observation without rancor or bitterness, but with a conviction borne of long experience. Even as I express it, however, I feel guilty of a certain ingratitude; for my treatment from the student press over the years has been generally satisfactory.

I would not have you think for a moment that I have been wholly spared. A dean or president who has not had his brushes with the campus yellow sheet simply has not done a good job. For even the most solid youthful citizen turns into something strange and frightening when he is chosen for an editorial or reportorial position and discovers for the first time the might of the pen. He may even resort to humor, a device which in his hands is painfully and consistently misguided. For example, on the very day when with fitting fanfare we were dedicating a new chemistry building, the funds for which had been donated by a kindly benefactor named Mr. *Old*house, the college paper came out with an April 1st headline dubbing it *"Out*house Hall." To say that we rushed frantically

111

into the breach is a bit of an understatement. Fortunately the donor proved to be more understanding than we might have expected.

Years ago I evolved a kind of standard operating procedure in my campus press relations. Whenever a new student editor is announced to the waiting public I issue a cordial invitation for him to join me for a spot of tea, a bit of sherry, or whatever is appropriate to the institution and the circumstances. After amiable congratulations I introduce my lecture with the personal doctrine that censorship of the student press is at least a cardinal if not a deadly sin. I then assure him (or her) that even if requested I will review material in advance with extreme reluctance.

On the other hand, as one of the officials responsible for the total welfare of the institution, I am equally firm in assuring him that I will peruse each issue with a critical eye and not hesitate to communicate my reactions forcibly, albeit always confidentially. I point out further that since the student paper usually bears the proud masthead of the college, it becomes perforce a quasi-official publication; that, unlike the public press, it is unique in its freedom from competition (except for an occasional underground sheet); that its student readers generally have no option but to contribute to its fiscal upkeep; and that for the most part and unlike the public press, it has been relatively free of court suits. When it is sued, moreover, the college and its hapless president are usually co-defendants with the editor. Thus it is in many ways a peculiarly privileged form of journalistic endeavor.

Under these circumstances, I explain, it has responsibilities which are also special. One of these, since the paper is usually *the* organ for the campus as a whole, is to represent as broad a spectrum of campus opinion as possible. In short, it should not be the exclusive medium for the biases of one editor or editorial board. Second, since it is associated with a truth-seeking institution, the paper has an even greater responsibility than the public media to ferret out the facts and to present them fairly. Thus I invite the editor and the staff whom he assigns to cover my office to feel free to ask me anything they wish about issues in which I have a concern. If I feel that I cannot give the information they seek and if they feel that

112

my stated reasons for withholding it are not valid, then they may blast away. In theory, at least, I can then feel equally free to blast back, though in practice I have scrupulously avoided doing so. Any such response merely tends to prolong and enlarge the issue. Although on several occasions I surreptitiously encouraged a third party to set the record straight, I have never myself raised written objections to any grotesquery involving me in the student press (or in the public press either).

When the brief and friendly conference finally comes to a close I cross my fingers and wait.

The simple truth is, no one has yet figured out what to do with the student press. It has more ups and downs than a funicular. The four-letter word was not, of course, invented by a student editor, nor indeed by the leader of the Berkeley Free Speech Movement; yet the woods are full of youthful pressmen who pounce upon it with all the eagerness of an Eve first discovering the apple. All parents are shocked as each child in turn, around the age of four and a half, comes up with one of the forbidden syllables. They generally treat these moments of infant discovery as a learning experience and work out some mutual accommodation. Why, fifteen or so years later, some of these same children feel obliged to relive the experience is almost as mysterious as why the public treats their delayed maturity with such manifestations of outrage. Unfortunately, the man in the middle is usually the college president. At such times he can indeed be thankful if he himself has exercised parsimony in using the four-letter expression, for it can provide a great emotional release if it has not otherwise been overspent.

There are really few ways to control the student press in today's academic world. Perhaps the most effective is to develop a department of journalism and give it overall responsibility. The paper thus becomes its official departmental laboratory. Inasmuch as the editor, under this arrangement, is usually someone who is pointing toward a career in journalism, he keeps a weather eye out for that final job recommendation from the department and handles the paper accordingly. Although this has never seemed quite cricket to me, it does make for a higher quality of journalistic achievement

113

and a greater degree of peace on the campus. Sooner or later such control will be challenged, usually by several of the militants in the English department, but in the meantime it can provide a relatively happy arrangement.

The more common means of control is through an all-college board of publications—an uneven device at best. If the president has been sufficiently shrewd or lucky, he can designate one or two of the more responsible faculty as his representatives on the board. Then when aberrations occur, as they invariably will, it is not the president but the board which withholds the funds from the paper or suspends the editor. The national collegiate journalism society (whose Greek-letter designation I can never remember) has developed a code of ethics. I first learned about it when, after a particularly offensive edition of the campus paper came to my attention, I proposed to the editor that he adopt the first two clauses in the Rotary Club's "Four-Way Test": (1) "Is it the truth?" and (2) "Is it fair to all concerned?" Little did I know! The editor and his staff raised violent objection, saying that their profession has its own code, thank you. Ah, well. . . .

A few years back several national associations, including the National Student Association and the Association of American Colleges (representing college presidents), issued a joint statement on student rights. With one of their recommendations in particular I was in profound disagreement—that the student paper become wholly independent of any segment of the college administration. In the years since the dissemination of this manifesto I have seen issues of student papers devoted blatantly to fomenting campus violence, or containing graphic front-page pictures of intercourse in the raw, or printing libelous attacks on administrators or faculty members. Although such enlightening news items tend to characterize the underground press, I am just old enough to believe that the above-ground student press should seek to emulate the highest rather than the lowest of journalistic standards . . . possibly *The Times* of London rather than *The Daily Express*. But since this wish is not likely to be father to the thought; and particularly since any administrative effort at supposed suppression of such journalistic vagaries

114

will automatically unite the support of all campus liberals and even some of the conservatives behind the students, I have pretty much come around to the belief that the student paper should have its umbilical firmly and cleanly severed. The paper should no longer carry the college name, should receive no funds through any institutionally managed source, and should be forced to survive on the willingness of its readers to pay for their subscriptions. In this manner it will stand or fall on its quality, interest, and acceptability; and the administration will be free of one of its otherwise insoluble problems.

So much for the student press. But one other word before I close.

A few months ago in unpacking some old books and papers I came across several issues of my own undergraduate "literary" journal. I naturally turned first to one of my own early ventures into the poet's corner. It began with a cheery, "A night of dark and gloom of deepest pall . . ." Frankly, I was too embarrassed to go on. Yet as I reflect on some of the more recent output of our campus literary artists, I don't think there has been too much improvement. Mankind may ultimately be perfectible, but I sometimes wonder about student writers. I suppose I had to grade entirely too many freshman themes in my day.

This doesn't mean I am irrevocably against student literary journals, if only they didn't have to be referred to as "literary"! Nor indeed do I find them substantially improved by the inclusion of fugitive pieces by members of the faculty, some of whom, if you will trouble to look, are listed elsewhere in the journal as its faculty advisers. I find such displays just a little pathetic.

Well, Stanley, old chap, I hear sounds of life elsewhere in our suite. Furthermore I haven't quite finished reading *The Times*. Until the next issue . . .

Cheerio,

C. J.

115

Dear Stanley:

I notice from our window this morning what the Londoners probably consider only a light dew. There are even a few chaps walking with their umbrellas furled—a sign of typical English understatement. So far as I am concerned, however, it is raining, and with the light case of sniffles which always greets me in this otherwise favorite city and since I shall soon bring these letters to a close, I want you just to settle back and let me spin a little fable-with-a-moral. Feel free to read it in as many installments as you wish, though it is something with at least a beginning and a middle, even if the end may yet be a little obscure.

I am moved to write to you about a subject that has been near to my heart for a number of years—the subtle but relentless pollution of institutional identity in our colleges and universities. I hope you will bear with me as I develop the case, for it is a matter of real concern to anyone aspiring to a position of high academic leadership.

Two quick assumptions before I launch into my text: first, I perceive the future of American higher education as imitating the present trends of American business—the development, in whatever configuration, of larger and larger systems. I care not whether we are talking about private or publicly supported institutions, for the difference is narrowing day by day. Second, I conceive of our academic structure as a continuum in which our present difficulties may be viewed as the suffering of sea changes, as symptoms of altering identity, on the way to some new and strange destinations.

116

To dramatize my assumptions I want to take you along with me to a wholly mythical monarchy known as Graustark, a charmed land whose complex systems of higher education are perhaps slightly atypical but nonetheless illustrative of the stern admonition in James Whitcomb Riley's "Little Orphan Annie," "The goblins will get *you* if you don't watch out."

Graustark boasts (1) a fair number of fine private colleges and universities, in which there already can be seen signs of self-protective grouping into larger configurations; (2) an expensive and distinguished university system; (3) a state college system which is even larger, though relatively far less expensive; and (4) a junior college system whose true dimensions are unknown to even the most couth of the nation's pundits. Since for obvious reasons I can clearly not embrace (an interesting term under the circumstances) the entire complex, let me limit our attention to that component which the natives proudly refer to as the Graustark State College System, or GSCS.

At last count (these figures, like the Dow Jones averages, change from day to day) the GSCS consists of twenty-three separately identifiable colleges, strategically placed (as dictated by unselfish political considerations) over the length and breadth of the country, each with its own president and yet affiliated under a single board of trustees and a central office, once affectionately known as the Empyrean because of its location on Empire Boulevard. The latter houses an official titled the chief warden, a passel of vice wardens, and heaven only knows how many other busy bureaucrats. The principle that ties the separate ganglia of the system together is known as "affiliation," a term which premises a large degree of independence in the component colleges and, following as night the day, a responsibility upon each single unit to maintain a strong institutional identity. Technically the separate branches of the University of Graustark are simply that—branches of a single entity. Each unit in the GSCS, on the other hand, is technically a separate entity confederated with the other twenty or so separate entities, perhaps out of some sort of primitive instinct for survival—and, in-

117

cidentally, as a supposed means of saving the taxpayers' dollars. Thus it provides a suitable laboratory in which to study the principles of institutional identity.

At this point I want to direct our attention to one particular campus in the GSCS—not the largest or smallest, not the oldest or newest, neither the best nor the worst, and thus perhaps one of the ideal subjects for study. In point of fact, it existed as a separate institution years before it was incorporated, about a decade ago, into this Hydra-headed system. In short, it once had a well-established identity. Its struggle now is to preserve what identity it may have left.

Identity implies at least a discernible modicum of independence, and we would be captious indeed if we did not recognize that, technically, the president and the faculty of our specimen college have a degree of self-determination. Within limits they can determine the curriculum, course schedules, and calendar. They design academic and physical master plans, subject, naturally, to approval from above. They make their own faculty and administrative appointments below the office of the president. They initiate their budget within the GSCS formulae and have the authority even to transfer funds among certain categories. They handle their own public relations, maintenance, and minor capital construction. Superficially their responsibilities are similar to those carried on in any independent college or university. The chief warden of the system, in fact, from time to time takes occasion to remind them and their colleagues in the other colleges that the system is indeed an *affiliation* of separate institutions. Moreover, some presidents have been known to rise in wrath when the central bureaucracy, advertently or otherwise, encroaches on local prerogatives. They postulate as the ideal an arrangement whereby the chief warden and his staff would (1) function merely as the lever to pry from the government an ever enlarging annual subsidy and (2) come to their aid in time of crisis—but only by invitation.

However, all is not so simple as it may appear. The struggle for identity in the rapidly growing GSCS is nothing short of desperate, and calls for constant vigilance. Further, because the pattern

118

of higher education in Graustark, if not throughout the world, is toward larger and larger systems, I believe that the following analysis, though limited for the most part to a single academic configuration, contains signs of "clear and present danger."

One of these dangers is local and intrinsic. Some of the GSCS presidents and their staffs tend to call on the central office for "hand-holding" not just in times of tribulation but even in the brief periods between crises, thus casting doubt upon their independent initiative and encouraging participation by the chief warden's staff in local decision making. Unfortunately, decisions reached in this manner tend to be precedent setting and to have systemwide implications. Thus the identity-seeking units themselves can be said to have let their birthright be garnisheed without too much awareness of what is happening. They are a little like Proust's man in the bath whose water heats from warm to scalding but so gradually that he never knows at quite what moment to scream.

A second force is at work here as well, a force that is hardly sinister but nonetheless destructive of institutional identity. The chief warden of the GSCS is quite adamant in his insistence on preserving the principle of affiliation and on the desirability of institutional identity and independence. At the same time, since the Graustarkians are human, the structure of his own office is ineluctably bureaucratic. Because the stakes are high—he and his staff are responsible for an annual systemwide budget of three hundred million krashas (one krasha is the rough equivalent of a 1970 American dollar)—he perforce surrounds himself with highly qualified top-echelon staff, men who are able and, it follows, ambitious. Under these men are subordinate staff officers who are also able and ambitious; and thus each unit in the headquarters office quite understandably tends to accumulate power. Although the office can and often does operate with the best intent in the world, the results are nevertheless a gradual accrual of centralized authority. What is more, this power has currency solely in terms of control over the colleges that compose the system, and every transfer of power to the central authority is subtracted from the independent identity of the constituent colleges.

119

The story is still not complete. Where public funds and the accountability for public funds are involved there are no utopias, not even in Graustark. Inevitably, somebody is bound to make a mistake. Whether it results from ineptness or criminal intent (fortunately rare) the outcome is predictable. Investigations are conducted and protective controls instituted. The innocent end up suffering with the guilty. Mistakes made on one campus eventuate in new controls imposed on all.

Let me illustrate. Historically, each college in the GSCS developed one or more independent, nonprofit foundations or corporations to handle such extra-budgetary interests as the bookstore, food services, contractual research, student unions, gifts and grants, and the like. To manage these functions, each campus devised formats compatible with the distinctive character of its locality. Some of these foundations, depending upon the age and size of the college, are relatively small; others manage annual operations in the millions. Some are governed by lay boards of local business leaders, some by faculty and administration, others by students, still others by combinations of the three.

Recently some serious shortcomings came to public notice. In one instance a foundation, through poor management, was discovered to be in arrears by eight hundred thousand krashas; in another, funds were allegedly diverted to a militant student—yes, there are militants even in Graustark—for the purchase of firearms. The government, which has always coveted the foundation funds lying just beyond its direct control, became understandably exercised. To the surprise of no one and in order to avert repressive legislative attention, the chief warden and the board quickly devised a new set of "guidelines" (a delightful euphemism) curtailing the independence of the foundations throughout the system and tending ultimately toward making them wholly indistinguishable. Thus another degree of institutional identity has been lost.

Perhaps so long as a single college within a conglomerate can maintain control over its academic personality, other forms of administrative templating could be viewed as irrelevant to institutional identity; but this presupposes that the academic and the fiscal are

120

separable. This they are not, never have been, and never can be. Faculty salaries, of course, in a system as large as the GSCS are based on a common scale and thus pose no particular problems to institutional identity. (They pose other problems, but none to institutional identity.) But when a particular college in the system seeks to evolve a unique academic program, which can well mean some tampering with student-faculty ratios, then the budget rears its fiscal head. A number of the GSCS colleges, responsive to the natural desire to be innovative, have tried from time to time to argue their right to special budgetary consideration. But let one receive such a concession! Immediately the other twenty or so campuses storm the Emypyrical ramparts with outcries of discrimination, buddyism, myopia, cranial softening, and the like. Although academic innovation is officially and enthusiastically encouraged, the system itself makes significant innovation next to impossible.

In any college or university a distinctive identity is difficult to achieve. In the GSCS the obstacle race is rare and wonderful to behold. Let us suppose that our dean awakes in the night with the dream of a revolutionary new program. Since administrators are not supposed to have ideas the dean will, if he is prudent, wait until dawn and then undertake to sell the concept to a member of the teaching staff who, pledged to secrecy and anxious to stay on the good side of the administration, will present it to his academic department as his own brainchild. If the department thinks it worthy, the proposal, after substantial modification, will advance to the curriculum committee of the school, the next largest administrative unit. If, in turn, it survives this harrowing dissection it will be passed to the all-college curriculum committee, which may after a political auto-da-fé recommend it to the dean—who will be lucky even to recognize it as his original brainchild. As the next step the good gentleman will consult with the president and then, assuming the latter's blessing, with the academic staff in the chief warden's office. By now we can assume that the original concept is thoroughly emaciated; but if it still has enough spark to survive rigorous evaluation in the Empyrean it would properly come before the trustees for their imprimatur.

121

But here I, and it, must pause. For institutional identity is vastly more involute in the GSCS than I have made it seem so far. Before the trustees can consider the most fleeting academic dream, particularly if it involves a substantive departure from established patterns, the systemwide academic council, a curious representative body, which is responsive to certain political forces to be discussed in a moment, will subject it to microscopic analysis, first through the agency of its standing committee on academic affairs, then its executive committee, and finally the council itself in plenary and solemn high convocation.

Because this council is a democratic agency whose delegates are tied by loyalty to their own institutional identities, it is likely to be concerned not so much with whether the proposal is educationally valid as with whether it will give one campus a fraction of preeminence over another. It will also scrutinize the proposal in terms of whether it in any way obliges the involved teaching staff to deviate from standard working conditions or implies an increase of administrative control over matters considered to be sacrosanct prerogatives of the faculty.

Meanwhile we can only guess at the degree of identity crisis back at the Pierian Springs from whence the proposal flowed. But believe me, everything so far has been done with only the highest good will and for the best interests of all! (Except possibly the students.)

Now let us assume that the statewide academic council and the GSCS trustees have approved the new program and that there is enough of it left to give the home team a modest degree of distinctive identity. Since we are dealing with a dream anyway, let us also assume that the proposal involves the establishment of a new administrative unit in our college, perhaps a school of invertebrate lunology. We know that there is already such a program at a branch of Graustark University and still another at the independently controlled Graustark Institute of Technology. We are positive, however, that ours is different in concept, that it serves a unique and vital need.

Gradually we begin to realize that we haven't seen anything

122

yet. For there are other very significant roadblocks between creative identity and fiscal reality in the Graustarkian system. The same legislative enactment which systematized the previously independent state colleges established the coordinating commission (known as BLOCU—Bureau for Leveling Ordinary Collegiate Utopias), a body whose function is to advise the government on *all* matters dealing with higher education, public and private, in the monarchy of Graustark. Its members consist of representatives of the private colleges and the three tax-supported systems and several members-at-large. For the most logical bureaucratic reasons in the world BLOCU has moved beyond its original mandate and now functions virtually as a decision-making, at times even a quasi-legislative, body. In fact it only recently voted "to set up a procedure whereby the academic master plan of both the university and the state colleges will be reviewed by the bureau first—before going to either segment's governing board." Thus it will obviously be quite concerned with our proposed new school, even before the GSCS trustees can get their crack at it. The more cynical might suspect that the proposal will get its hearing before BLOCU not so much on its merits as on whether it impinges on the interests of one or more of the other systems represented in the bureau. BLOCU in this instance would have the power to lay the already battered and worn dream quietly to rest, buried beneath great mounds of mimeograph paper.

Again, however, let us dream that it has passed even this barrier. Surely now that creative little dean back home can begin counting her chickens. Unfortunately, no. There exists still another hurdle, the monolithic Graustarkian department of finance. Even the lowest functionaries in this august agency have power to make chief wardens and presidents quiver with apprehension. Against this Gibraltar has foundered many a brilliant design for institutional identity.

Well, this recital is becoming a little oppressive. Let me brashly assume that the Department of Finance has, mirabile dictu, given assent and, sneaking our proposal past the emperor's watchful aides, garbed it in budgetary raiment for legislative approval. The legislative analyst, a noble spirit whose responsibility is to save the

123

empire as much money as possible, is nevertheless sympathetic and has urged it upon the committees on educational affairs, finance, and ways and means. Finally it seeps out of committee to the floor of both houses (in this citadel where a house is definitely not a home) and, since this is fiction, emerges trailing clouds of tax krashas, in promissory notes, behind it.

Back home all is in readiness for celebration. Suddenly, however, a message arrives that the emperor, having grasped for the first time that implementation of this program would cost thirty-five thousand krashas in the initial year alone (in a budget of a mere five or so billion), had sternly blue-penciled the item, thus dashing the hopes of a lot of earnest little searchers after academic identity.

I recently heard Logan Wilson, head of the American Council on Education, express apprehension over the tendency in American higher education to add more and more levels between the "firing line" of the individual campus and the offices or agencies where final educational determinations are made. Obviously this has already happened in Graustark. Thus I can find it in my heart to be sorry for the college administrators who are the targets of student and faculty militants, not to mention aroused taxpayers, and yet who actually have minimal control over what happens around them. They may dream their dreams but they are powerless to enact their actions. Their lives would be much simpler and their institutional identities more easily preserved, of course, if they could be left to their own devices. However, in Graustark, as in the United States, walls cannot be erected around the campus (though fences have been seriously proposed).

I have not analyzed all of the forces, inside or out, which make it difficult for the individual institution in our growing academic systems to maintain a distinctive identity. I will bypass as only partially germane the whole question of student and faculty unrest, and yet it is a major factor in creating the image of a campus and in making one field of battle resemble another.

Students of institutional identity point out still another potenially destructive force. For many years now it has been well known in Graustark that the faculty member's devotion to his academic discipline has tended to erode loyalty to his institution. His ambition is often more in the direction of seeking greater visibility in, say, the world of economics than in rising within the academic ranks in his own college. He assumes, quite rightly in most cases, that promotion in rank, particularly in large systems, is primarily a function of the aging process. In the GSCS, more perhaps than in any other similar confederation, another form of extraterritorial distraction works against institutional loyalty and identity. I refer to the existence of five distinct and sporadically warring faculty organizations, similar to the American Association of University Professors, the State Employees Association, the College and University Faculty Association, the Association of State College Professors, and the American Federation of Teachers. Each has a branch or chapter on each GSCS campus and maintains a central secretariat which designs policies and programs affecting the whole. It is only too obvious that to the extent any one of these groups can command the loyalties of its constituency, to that extent the identity of the individual college is compromised. Through their publications and the occasional direct intervention of their officials, one or more of these organizations is constantly seeking to intervene in matters affecting local autonomy, even to wresting control of the statewide academic council.

Thus the individual college in the GSCS is buffeted from within and without, by students and faculties, by unions and the news media, by senates and trustees, by the coordinating bureau and the emperor. Little wonder if the thoughtful observer should relapse into the mood of Matthew Arnold's "Dover Beach," where ignorant armies clash by night. In such a mood he might rightly ask whether institutional identity is but a pipe dream in the ever enlarging educational systems which, I repeat, bode well to become the organizational wave of the future.

The problem for many private colleges, particularly those of recent vintage, is how to *achieve* identity; the problem for the GSCS college is how to *preserve* identity. Even in architectural patterns the critical visitor can find on various of the older campuses identical and hideous red brick dormitories designed, according to legend,

125

by a specialist in penal architecture. Fortunately for the institutional identity of one GSCS campus located in an area of moderate rainfall the bricks were discovered to admit moisture and thus were permitted to be adorned with gray waterproof paint; but for the most part the only distinctiveness has come from the creative planting of ivy. So far no systemwide regulations have been designed to cover this activity, possibly because those involved are still relatively too green.

In fairness it must be said that the newer campuses in the GSCS have been provided with their own architectural vocabulary; but, in the next breath, we must add that all such artistic decisions are made by the central architectural staff and the trustees, not by the home team. Moreover, rigid space formulas and budgetary restrictions have somewhat the same kind of standardizing effect as does the present requirement that all orders over twenty-five krashas go through the government's central purchasing agency. (This represents approximately 82 per cent of the value of all purchase requisitions initiated by each of the colleges in the GSCS and the chief warden's office as well.) With every operation preaudited, audited, and postaudited; with the most elaborate reports of every conceivable kind required not only by the headquarters office, the coordinating bureau, the department of finance, and the government and even by the saints above, reports which are often subject to on-campus review by off-campus inspectors, is there any wonder that the individual campus feels at times immured in a Kafkaesque castellation?

Moreover, the presidents of all colleges in the system are required to meet regularly with the chief warden; the academic vice-presidents of each college meet with the academic vice warden; the business officers with the financial vice warden. The deans of students, the admissions officers and registrars, the directors of research, even the student body presidents are organized into systemwide cadres for meetings with their central office counterparts and soon, it may be conjectured, with their counterparts from the BLOCU as well. Institutional identity? Well, if there is a law of the excluded

126

muddle in the logic of institutional integrity one might readily predict what the exclusion is likely to be.

The situation is grim. It is not, however, hopeless.

It is my conviction, Stanley, that the only hope of rising above the common denominator lies in the quality of leadership provided by the faculty and more particularly by those primi inter pares, the deans and the presidents. At a time when, in the conception of a Clark Kerr, the president is in danger of becoming a mere consensus taker, such leadership is becoming rare indeed. Yet to me it seems almost axiomatic that the greatest possibility for nurturing the precious flower of institutional identity lies in identfying and attracting the strongest possible leadership. I see these women and men as the kinds who can inspire (I originally wrote "fire") the faculty and students with dreams of institutional greatness; who can interpret the purposes of the college to a public grown increasingly apprehensive and confused over the seeming irresponsibility of the academic world; who can operate effectively in the multifaceted political area; men and women whose iron constitutions can preserve them in office long enough for at least a minimal degree of academic accomplishment. Cherchez l'homme! Or, in this day of Women's Liberation, cherchez la femme!

Yours in the holy quest,

Parsifal Coltswood, Esq.

Dear Stanley:

The subject I am moved to discourse on this morning has no relevance to the campus where we have been enjoying a day or two of most gracious hospitality. We are staying in the old manor house, which is allegedly haunted by the ghost of the hapless Lady Sneyd. Let me observe merely that to our not inconsiderable disappointment, her troubled spirit must have rested the night through. We did not hear so much as a single clanking chain. (Marj just observed that the manor house itself, after dark, makes belief in spirits quite easy.)

On more than one occasion on this "sentimental journey" we have found ourselves in discussions with Europeans who were quite critical of the United States because of our treatment of the racial minorities, criticism which is certainly more than justified. My defense—and I fell very easily into a posture which some might call chauvinistic—was that no European who did not have great familiarity with the United States could understand the scope of the problem or the degree of effort with which we were seeking solutions. I would then add, if that did not do it, that we had no corner on the market for discrimination and racial prejudice and that in my admittedly superficial investigations I saw little evidence in the several European countries on our itinerary of any effort to combat same.

By the time you, Stanley, become a college president the problem of discrimination on campus, particularly the racial variety, may have been solved, though, realistically, I'm certain neither you nor I will live that long. Not even the most sensitive, unprejudiced, sympathetic chief executive can escape the dimensions of the problem these days. Nor despite his best efforts is he likely to avert feelings of the most profound frustration. Thus these letters would be incomplete without some address to the subject.

Regardless of their academic backgrounds, few deans and even fewer presidents are philosophers, let alone psychologists or sociologists. Their lives are too quickly swallowed up in the morass of pragmatism. Thus if you wish to probe in depth into the causes and cures of racial prejudice on campus, I can assure you that there is no dearth of material. I can assure you also that very little of it has been written by administrators. They have been much too preoccupied with trying to confront the problem and to save their institutions from destruction.

On the theory that history can and occasionally does repeat, I think you may profit somewhat, Stanley, by a brief account of how this problem can evolve. (I hope I do not sound too professorial.) Let me take you to an imaginary private college in an area not too far removed from high concentrations of at least two minority groups, blacks and those of Spanish descent. Because of its high tuition it has had relatively few students over the years from either of these groups. There were always some, however, and the college consciously treated them no differently from the rest of the students. Nor was it particularly conscious of any injustice in the fact that they represented so small a percentage of the total student body. After all, the minorities merely had to meet the entrance requirements and present a valid claim upon the school's not unlimited scholarship resources. There were always a number of blacks on the football and basketball teams, and the results were highly satisfactory; but few persons thought of the players as anything but athletes.

But bit by bit the conscience of the country, and particularly of the campus, began to stir awake. The first in the administration to become sensitive to the discrepancies between policy and practice were the admissions officers. The first in the faculty, naturally enough, were from the liberal extreme in the social sciences and humanities departments. Then one day, several years back during a summer session, four or five of the faculty and one admissions offi-

129

cer were colloguing in the faculty dining room. Out of this grew a
rather poorly defined but nonetheless sincere "Equal Opportunity
Program." To their great credit, the initiators gave generously
of their time both to recruiting a small group of disadvantaged
students and to providing counseling and tutoring to assure the students' successful adjustment to academic life. The college even managed, at this late date, to salvage some funds from its shallow scholarship pool to meet the students' financial needs. A majority of the
initial group of students, even though few met the conventional
standards of admission, managed to survive into the second semester. The president, dean, and involved faculty were feeling all of
the satisfaction of the righteous.

But this was a college, and in a college everything is more
complicated than it seems at the outset. The first complication came
when a few faculty members from the conservative faction bruited
it abroad that they had asked to participate but were excluded by
the "fuzzies" who had "taken the program over." The accusation
was quickly and heatedly rebutted: "We asked them to help, but
they all claimed they were too busy." The acrimony, true to its nature, grew more bitter.

At about this time the federal government inaugurated the
Work Study and the Equal Opportunity programs, both designed
to provide funds for enlarging educational opportunities for disadvantaged students, particularly from the minority groups. The administration of the college sought and obtained federal funds to
enlarge its program substantially for the second and third years; and
this should have satisfied everybody. In expectation of the increase
a director of the program was sought and minority representation
was added to the student personnel and the financial-aid staffs. How
could anything go wrong with a design so well intentioned as this!

Well, it was quickly discovered that personnel qualified in
minority problems were both rare and in great demand. Every college and university in the area was vigorously competing in the same
limited market. Although *this* was not altogether unexpected, several
totally unexpected things did occur. The first of these was that the
minority students in the program, with or without encouragement

from their faculty supporters, declared that they and they alone were capable of judging who the director and staff should be; and the administration was confronted with an emotionally charged situation which quickly added to the polarization on the campus. As a result, when the director was chosen, even though he was a member of one of the two principal minorities and even though he was a man of at least modest talents, he was instantly ground between two almost irreconcilable forces. His devotion to the cause of improving the educational thrust of the disadvantaged was unfortunately not matched by his administrative skills; and when, as happened on one or two occasions during his brief tenure, he tried to do something on his own initiative, the student-faculty committee, which dominated the program, quickly set him straight.

At about this same time also it was discovered that, quite independent of the admissions office, a number of students from the committee paid visits to high schools in the college's service area and promised numbers of minority students not only a place in the next entering class but full financial assistance. Quantity, not quality, was the prime consideration. The college admissions staff was rightly upset; the high school guidance officers were no less so. When the president firmly pointed out to the student-faculty committee that there were no such funds available, the students threatened to picket his office until he found the money. Believing in the overt objectives of the program, he promised to seek public donations and did in fact initiate a drive for funds. On the day he made a public announcement of the drive, with pledges already in hand from a half dozen leading citizens, a number of students in the program, with an assist from the campus Students for a Democratic Society, staged a demonstration which, naturally, made the headlines in the press. Since TV cameras were on hand, this was the obvious intent. Thereafter, not one additional cent was raised from private sources for minority financial aid.

Up to this point the program had developed on the base of a considerable amount of donated time from both faculty and administration. The selfless faculty sponsors decided, however, that they should be paid extra for their services, or at least be given credit in the form of released time from their regular course assignments. Although this was not an unreasonable request, it added further to the costs of the underbudgeted program and more fuel to the fires in those departments that felt the program was not only highly suspect academically (as indeed it was) but a drain as well on already limited faculty positions.

As if this were not enough, the committee came up with a new statement of policy and a design calling for a summer institute for all students entering the program in the fall. The ostensible purpose was orientation. To the critics it seemed more like indoctrination. Attendance was to be mandatory, even though the actual educational design was vaguely formulated and, as it turned out, anything but successful. The students, a number of whom had to give up well-paying summer jobs, were understandably resentful.

Further, the document prepared and distributed by the committee suggested that the process of selection of minority students for the program should take favorable account of militant activity in high school or even junior high. And while there was a logic in their position, which I will not take the time to uncover here, the impact upon the conservative faction among the faculty and community was easily predictable. It was claimed that an intelligent, nonmilitant student had little chance for acceptance. A concerted effort was made to scuttle the entire program, an effort that would have been successful except for the administration's determination to maintain some sort of viable educational opportunity for disadvantaged students. The program was temporarily saved, but it limped badly as the new year progressed.

On a nearby campus, which was experiencing similar agonies, the two principal minority groups began to fight each other for control of the EOP program. Inevitably, the shock waves moved outward. With the forced resignation of the first director in midyear, they became quite discernible. Months of wrangling were spent in seeking a new director acceptable to both of the principal minority groups, as well as to the president, who was beginning to feel like the minorest minority of them all.

Compromise candidates are a frequent reality in political

life, and in campus politics as well. They are sometimes even effective in office. In this instance the successful candidate's honeymoon period was glorious. A few people were even overheard giving forth sighs of relief. It looked as if the minority student was at last going to have an opportunity to pursue an education that could be tailored to his individual needs; in short, that he would not be either the victim of the do-gooders or a pawn in an awesome game of power politics for as yet undisclosed ends.

The rest of the story will have to be interpreted in accordance with one's own orientation. If you believe that the objectives of higher education are to bring about major social change and that these can be achieved only through a kind of organized separatist movement, then the next year or so at our model campus was highly successful. A dormitory was set aside for the EOP students, with the clear understanding that federal law prohibited its being limited to racial minorities. Unfortunately, it proved in fact to be so limited: after the first few weeks, no white student roomed in the dormitory during the period in which it served as the "Educational Opportunity Center." Members of the faculty and administration, apart from those from the two principal minorities, were made to feel distinctly unwelcome.

An ethnic studies department was established, with the highest expectations. A long list of nontraditional courses was designed by the participants, forwarded to the liberal-dominated curriculum committee, and given skeptical approval by the faculty. In addition to cultural histories (in one or two instances taught by student leaders who had miraculously acquired expertise in the field) there were courses in the literature of militancy, soul food, how to beat the establishment, and the black athlete. The successful completion of a sufficient number of these was to be recognized by the awarding of the baccalaureate. The question of what the recipient would have that was marketable was tentatively raised but quickly silenced by the minority student spokesmen, who were always sensitive to the slightest evidence of unenthusiasm.

It became increasingly evident that the individual minority student had little independence from his own student and faculty

133

leaders. He was directed where and when to appear for meetings and demonstrations. Stories of threats and intimidation reached the ears of the administration. Threats were even made against the president himself, who was openly accused of racism and of seeking to subvert the program. Close ties were clearly discernible with activists on other campuses and in the larger community. Protest marches inevitably included individuals who could not be identified by members of the student personnel department.

The next stage was easily predictable. An opposition group of students and faculty organized themselves, and on one or two occasions violent confrontation was narrowly averted. Less responsible individuals from each camp conceived a variety of ingenious ways to vent their feelings on the other; and while this had the effect of temporarily reuniting the two principal minority groups, it easily persuaded the president and dean that they were indeed sitting on the rim of a volcano. This feeling was scarcely dispelled by a rash of small fires on campus, the fire-bombing of one of the major buildings, and an attempt to destroy the records in the registrar's office.

On this imaginary campus and on many another campus throughout the United States and the world, at the time of this writing, the situation I have just described is all too real. Few administrators can look down the road with unalloyed optimism. A great deal of blame has been directed against college and university leadership for its failure to deal with campus violence with sufficient vigor; and some of this blame is justified. Unfortunately, the president has to operate within a frame of reference which, by and large, was not of his making but is nonetheless inflexible. The student militants focus upon him because he is the symbol of authority in a society from which they feel alienated. Their attitudes, however, are much easier to understand than those of the faculty, whose failure in many instances to insist upon responsible and mature deportment on the part of their colleagues is often at the heart of campus disruption.

Yet there is some reason for hope. There are mounting signs of greater willingness among top administration to confront the forces of disruption and on the part of faculty to play a more responsible role in assuring orderly campus procedures. Even more promising, I detect recently a new awareness on the part of students that violence is counterproductive and that they have all too often been the unwitting dupes of those who would destroy our society by first destroying its most essential, and yet most fragile agencies, its colleges and universities.

I offer these vaguely hopeful observations, my dear Stanley, not out of a desire to join the ranks of the seers and haruspices but rather because anyone who lingers long in the academic world, particularly if he be a dean or president, must be basically an optimist—or else!

Hopefully yours,
Charles

Dear Stanley:

As I sit here on the bank of the Ouse in the heart of Yorkshire it's a little difficult to feel cantankerous; and yet, since the few Yorkshiremen I have known claim that cantankerousness is basic to the character of this area, one is almost obliged to get into the spirit of the thing. Particularly because I have scarcely been able to pick up a newspaper in recent weeks without reading something more about the desirability of student involvement in collegiate affairs, I want to "cantanker" on this theme for a spell.

The Duke of Edinburgh is for greater student involvement; the Hart Committee at Oxford University is for greater student involvement; the new (now ex) U.S. Commissioner of Education, Dr. James E. Allen, is for greater student participation; President Nixon is for greater student participation. All college students are for greater student participation, and *I* am for greater student participation. In fact, these days you are an absolute nobody if you are not for greater student participation. But what does it mean and where is it leading?

In the first place, our public oracles seem to feel that this is something new. Any historian could point out, however, that our modern universities virtually began because a group of individuals called students, needing some kind of academic certification, managed to scrape up enough money to hire someone to cook for them and then, as things developed, they decided that an educated cook was better than a noneducated one and they began to hire their own faculty. For a variety of reasons, including the need to protect the professioriat against physical abuse from disaffected students, this

136

degree of participation was modified somewhat over the centuries, and there was a period of time when student involvement was confined largely to athletics, riots, and the regurgitation of goldfish. But for many decades now, and particularly since the return of the more mature veterans to the campus after World War II, there has been substantial and meaningful student participation in the formulation of university policies and in many forms of decision making.

But let's look outside of the university for a moment. In the last presidential campaign and perhaps to a greater degree than in any previous presidential campaign in the history of our country, college students became involved. The campaign results suggest that their involvement was almost totally disavowed. For three decades now our college-age youth have been very much involved in the security of this country, and yet not once have they been given any effective voice in decision making. The previous president of the United States and the present incumbent have come out in favor of reducing the voting age to eighteen, which would certainly provide for the possibility of more effective involvement. Congress has approved it. Yet in a number of states it has been voted down. Essentially there have been no major decisions of public policy, let alone of private policy, in our total American society in which the college-age youth have been invited actively to participate.

Some six years ago several things became rather evident. First, college students were discovered to be a maneuverable group with a tremendous potential for social change. Second, the group itself began to express discontent with its alienation from the centers of social power. Because it was not easy to revolt against society at large, they struck out against the nearest and most convenient agency, the university itself. The very fact, moreover, that the ostensible issues in so many of these rebellious episodes cover the widest possible range of subjects suggests that the issues themelves may not be so important as the generally unarticulated and perhaps not even well understood desire on the part of our youth to play a more meaningful role in society.

The overemphasis on college education in America keeps our young men and women from adulthood longer and longer each year. As more and more students go on to graduate school this delaying process goes on apace. One cannot help feeling at times that the process is deliberately extending a form of protective custody. Now we are confronted with increasing demands on the part of our students for greater participation in running our colleges—when in point of fact what they want and need and should have is greater participation in the major decisions of our society. At the same time we hear persons in high places calling upon the colleges and universities to give these students a larger role in university management—when what these individuals should be espousing is a format whereby our youth can be made to feel more significant in the total social structure.

But let's look at this popular rallying cry and see what it actually means.

Let me say at the outset that I favor the widest possible consultation with students in all matters affecting their academic, social, and even moral interests. As I may have observed in an earlier letter, it takes far less time to touch bases than to mend fences. I would go even a step beyond consultation and endorse the idea of students actually participating by discussion and vote in the formulation of policy, particularly when the policy relates to areas of their competence and interest—broadly rather than narrowly conceived. Anyone who disagrees with this does so at his own peril. But what are some of these areas of particular student competence?

One of the most salutary movements of the day is the determination of many undergraduate groups to play a role in the evaluation of the faculty. After all, the student is evaluating his instructor day in and day out; the only question is whether the instructor recognizes the fact and cares to know the results. Moreover, the whole process of evaluating teaching effectiveness is so unscientific that such additional input should always be welcomed—as long as it is not ultimately determinative. When, as in many institutions, it includes the widest possible student participation and the most sophisticated methodology, it comes close to being one of the best measures of teaching competence yet to be devised.

I would place slightly lower on the totem pole of priorities student participation in curricular determination, while still claiming for it substantial value. I have heard some instructors proudly claim that they design each course around what the students, through participatory democracy, decide they wish to study; and in some instances this may indeed be better than what the instructor himself might have determined. A new college in New England (I assure you it could never happen in Old England) seems to have based its total curriculum on this principle. My problem in such instances is to rationalize why the students should be expected to pay tuition or the instructor should expect to draw a salary. If he does not exercise at least some visible leadership and bring to the class some form of expertise, he would appear to be denying the validity of his own scholarly preparation. On the other hand, I suspect that the only way we shall counteract hardening of curricular arteries is through the massive infusion of direct student interest, even if we have to go on using the repulsive word "relevance."

But—and as any student of Shakespeare's *Othello* surely knows, "but" is the cruelest word in the English language—I have certain serious reservations about student participation.

In the first place, as I have just observed, students have been participating for countless college generations. The most obvious and traditional form is "student government." Whether or not, as today's militants would aver, student government is a "Mickey Mouse" operation, generally tolerated or even encouraged as a subtle means of administrative control over student affairs, is a matter of opinion. Going beyond opinion, it is nonetheless true that participation in student government has a rather dismal record. If 25 per cent of the total student body actually take the trouble to vote in any student election, this is a cause for unusual rejoicing. Even balloting on major and controversial issues scarcely brings out student voters in great numbers. While honor systems may perhaps seem a little old-fashioned in today's world, I recall not many years back when an energetic and idealistic cadre of students on my campus was vitally concerned with the establishment of just such a code of moral uplift. Innumerable hours were spent in committee sessions to limit the code to those areas which presumably would have the

139

greatest potential for initial success. A comparable effort was devoted to working out the details involved in establishing the system. It was agreed, after many a wrangle, that a 66.6-per cent positive vote was essential if the new system were to work.

When the day arrived, every conceivable technique was used to get the students to the ballot boxes. As a result an almost unprecedented turnout of 75 or so per cent was achieved. What is more, 66.2 per cent voted to adopt the system. At this point the student committee retired into an all-night session to consider whether or not to falsify the figures to bring them up to the agreed-upon minimum of 66.6. To their lasting credit in my book, they announced the results truthfully and the honor system was lost, presumably in perpetuity.

Normally a 25 per cent vote on any campus is considered to be better than par, as is a 25 per cent annual participation in all organized student activities. I interpret this as meaning, in effect, that when we talk of student participation, we generally are talking about at the most one quarter of the students. Of this quarter, only the smallest fraction represents the active leadership.

Even this fact should not be construed as necessarily a negative. The real problem with student participation lies elsewhere. In the first place, the students who come into positions of leadership through the elective or even the appointive process are not necessarily the leaders of student opinion. The opinion makers all too often are not interested in the hard, and to them infantile, labor of conducting a campaign. All one has to do is look at the penguin-like process by which consensus seems to be reached in convocations of the "out" generation. In the neo-romanticism which dominates so many campus movements, sentiment seems to have replaced rational debate and sequential monologue masquerades under the false term of "dialogue."

In the second place, having successfully forced faculty into including students in their deliberative bodies, I have spent entirely too many hours in meetings where the students either remained totally silent or came out with the most immature sorts of proposals. Their mere physical presence is not only meaningless, it is often counterproductive. Unless they are willing really to do their homework, they would do better staying in their rooms devoting a modicum of attention to their other homework. Perhaps the students' own perception of these shortcomings underlies some of today's campus militancy. Instead of governance by consultation many campus leaders seem to find it easier to strive for governance by confrontation. In one sense, I really do not blame the students for their feelings of frustration—though, as you could gather, Stanley, I conceive such student reaction to be at least in part the outcome of their own ineffectuality. They so often claim that they have tried all the normal channels without success and therefore must resort to more drastic measures.

Although I never thought of myself as a militant, I have equally never forgotten the experience of being a member of a small group of campus leaders in my undergraduate years who ultimately succeeded in exacting a promise from the president of the college that he would replace the fossilized academic dean and the hopelessly Victorian dean of women. Although we had no candidate for the latter position, the president agreed to place a certain faculty member in the former position effective at the opening of the new school year. This was on a Friday afternoon preceding commencement on Sunday. As I later ascertained, he did in fact speak with our candidate on the very next day, Saturday, and offered him the position. On Sunday afternoon I graduated, as did most of our "dissident" group. Monday morning when the president went to his office he found that his key no longer unlocked his door. Returning home to the presidential manse, he received a call from the chairman of the board informing him that he had been relieved of office. One of the junior students in our group, unquestionably the most brilliant scholar to have come to the institution in many years, was subsequently denied membership in Phi Beta Kappa; one of the others, a more marginal student (who nevertheless became a millionaire), was, oddly enough, discovered a day or two before his graduation to have some irregularities in his record and was never awarded the degree.

I fully recognize that this episode is rather extreme. I am

141

even willing to suggest that there were other factors in the situation about which we students could well have been ignorant. But I am afraid that often there are valid reasons for the feelings of frustration which are all too current in campus life. Many of these could be avoided, in part or wholly, through the process of honest and thoughtful consultation. To say, moreover, that the student is but a transient and therefore should not expect to participate in matters affecting the future of the institution is simply not an adequate response.

Equally, to complain about the amount of time required to break in each new student generation to a participatory role is specious. For one of the important functions of an academic community is to provide opportunities for the kind of learning experience which the student as citizen must engage in when he becomes an active member of the larger community.

As any administrator or parent has discovered, growing pains can at times be acute. Not long ago, one of my presidential colleagues introduced me, in passing, to an attractive young lady president of the student body. He asked her to come to his office that afternoon; and then, when she walked away, he explained what was going on. In their eagerness to try to help the college, which characteristically was having financial difficulties, several of the student leaders had communicated directly with certain federal agencies to solicit financial support. Although it was not impossible that their unsophisticated approach—they had done very little homework—might have produced results, what they did not know was that the college, through important national contacts, was already engaged in conversations with the same agencies. The president was properly concerned with untangling the wires.

One of my friends, president of a fine liberal arts college, has proposed a new kind of social contract in which each component of the academic community, while pledging all support to the well-being of the institution as a whole, is accorded certain participatory rights and responsibilities. This would negate the one-man-one-vote procedures which have been adopted, with extravagant claims, at a few institutions. It would presumably make a distinction between policy formulation and decision making. It would recognize levels of involvement and responsibility. It would both proscribe and prescribe. It would establish new principles of consideration, decency, integrity, and accountability. Anyway, there is no harm in dreaming, is there?

So there, Stanley, you have it for what it is worth. I defy any Yorkshireman in the immediate environs to outdo my native cantankerousness—or to zig as facilely as I have zagged.

Cordially,

C. F.

Dear Stanley:

Not only all good things but some not so good as well must come to an end. Now past the midpoint of this most welcome leave of absence, I am about to turn my energies to the thing which I told you most college and university presidents are forced to relinquish—the pleasure of conducting research in their academic discipline. Since I don't believe I can be any more successful in psychologically blending the two functions of administration and research at this stage in life than I was in the early years when I tried to combine teaching and deaning, I'm going to close these ruminations in a manner even more random than has been my style heretofore. In the odds and ends of notes I jotted during our travels I find a few ideas I need to chew on before I try to concentrate on the "Linguistic Eccentricities of *Troilus and Cressida*." Bodleian, here I come—after a few parting shots.

First, an observation or two on campus morale. As you know, Stanley, I have been in college or university administration for thirty years. I have never known a season when someone has not said to me, "Morale on this campus has never been at a lower ebb." And he was always right, for that is the divine nature of the beast. Morale, I feel certain, was created to be at low ebb. The wise administrator knows this and takes it in his stride. If it is not student morale, it will be faculty morale at the nadir. That administrative morale is at times less than ankle high is considered to be irrelevant. But just remember the old military adage: "An army which is not complaining is in danger of defeat." Be sympathetic, therefore, but

144

never dismayed. Every successful president must operate with a sense of history.

Totally unrelated to this last, I want to record for your abiding edification a few of my cherished notions on "innovation." When I am finally forced into retirement I intend to study the genesis of new ideas in academia—as well as the strategy and tactics of their implementation. Though past the age of maximum creativity, I nevertheless cling to the belief that significant curricular innovation springs as often from the academic administration as from the professoriat. Even if new data were to suggest the contrary I will never be convinced: for administrators who survive learn early that the only hope for the gestation of their brainchildren is strategic deception. I recall one of my own more brilliant conceptions which, since by this time I had had some seasoning, survived only because I browbeat a faculty friend (administrators occasionally have faculty friends) to peddle it as his own. After months of committee debate, during which I would from time to time cautiously plug in to assure myself that they were still on track, the proposal came before the total faculty and was overwhelmingly adopted. But not unanimously, for by this time the news of its origin had leaked. One of my more mature colleagues was overheard saying, "I would have voted for it except that it came from the dean!"

Regardless of the source, new ideas must have administrative support at the right moment if they are to survive. At one university where I inherited, administratively, an absolutely brilliant program, a program which combined educational with fiscal virtues, the only thing that enabled it to survive was grim determination on the part of the president and dean. The difficulty was that the innovation involved an entirely different concept of the utilization of faculty energies and time. One particularly brilliant professor was asked on a bibulous occasion why he didn't volunteer for the program. His reply was both candid and significant: "Why should I? I have things pretty soft the way they are!" His reaction suggests that the professorial "establishment" is so designed as generally to militate against substantial change in the status quo.

And this is one of the many reasons, Stanley, why I could predict that unionism will gain an ever stronger foothold over academic professionalism. On the surface the union issue seems to be related to salaries. I am strongly committed to the need for more tangible recognition of the services of our profession to the commonweal. But salaries have risen significantly in recent years (what hasn't!); yet the forces of unionism continue to grow all the stronger. As other industries strive to become more efficient and more productive (an invidious comparison, perhaps), we seem to strive for fewer hours and smaller classes. Last night, here in Oxford, I heard a story about the old don who when asked about his teaching load replied, "Oh, yes, I am still teaching! I lecture once a year, some years!" The premise that smaller classes and lighter teaching loads make for better learning is as yet unproven. Possibly they do, but we as a profession have devoted very little creative energy to evaluating our effectiveness. Perhaps this is what gives substance to the aphorism that the chief responsibility of the president and his dean is to "afflict the comfortable."

This defense of the status quo is also one of the many reasons why I would predict that student power and faculty power are sailing on a collision course. Despite the fact that much of our current campus unrest seems to focus upon the administration, a principal cause is unquestionably the lack of challenge in the classroom and laboratory. And this is one reason why students are demanding to serve on faculty committees and senates and why, in a few of the more alert institutions, students are conducting their own independent studies of the curriculum and demanding a share in evaluating the faculty. Here they are treading on the sacred ground of faculty prerogative. When they insist on a voice in appointments and promotions they are directly challenging the very core of faculty power. And as I sit here in one of the greatest centers of learning in the Western world, my candid administrative reaction is, "So much the better, and may the best man win!" I may feel differently when I get back home.

This leads me to a mild complaint. I hope, Stanley, that by the time you become a dean or president things will have changed, but I doubt they will. It seems to me that the usual campus is divided among (1) the research scholars whose pursuit of their mission allows for minimal interest in the institution, (2) the hibernators who never miss a class but whose classes would never miss them, and (3) the turks, young and old, who seem to think that campus political activity is an adequate substitute for scholarly responsibility. I am always pleasantly surprised when, among the three, we manage to end the year more or less in one piece. But is it any wonder that the natives (the students) have become restive?

As the lady said about the dictionary, it would be much more interesting if the subject didn't change so often! But I now want to report the results of a private survey I have casually made over the years. To wit, only a small portion of the students on any but the smallest campus know even the name of their college president, let alone recognize His Gray Eminence when they pass him on the mall. It may well be that he deliberately follows Bolingbroke's practice in *Richard II* of not allowing himself to be too common a sight to the eyes of la rozza multitudine. Even where he makes the most herculean efforts to be available to the students, however, the president still comes in contact with only a relative few. Thus I have never known a campus where the students didn't complain about the president's lack of interest in their interests. My only advice, dear Stanley, is to do your thing and not worry about the criticism you are bound to get anyway.

A besetting problem, of course, is that of the incessant demands upon the president and even the dean to be off campus. Recently, in response to a national survey, the results of which I still have not seen, I computed my absence from the campus for the past academic year at forty-five working days—and these did not, of course, include any of this glorious leave-of-absence. I pay a price and presumably the institution pays a price for these absences. But even the least seemingly essential ones have many tangible and intangible values. They help combat lurking cynicism and help me keep intellectually alive. Moreover, the campus is often quieter when the president is away. Half the fun is gone when the student agitators can't picket the symbol of authority. I remember one occasion when, in fact, I had delayed an announced vacation because of student unrest on campus. On the second day I received a delegation consisting of the chairman of the faculty senate, the student body president, and two top members of my administrative staff. Their common message was for me to pack my bags and leave. My continued presence, they explained, was interpreted both as a victory for the militants and a lack of confidence in the rest of the campus leadership. And so I lived to fight another day!

When Herman Hickman became head coach at Yale, he stated that his goal was "to keep the alumni surly but not mutinous." Which brings me to the next, and penultimate, topic in this dwindling potpourri: the president and the alumni. Since the main function of a college is to turn them out, the chief executive has an innate interest in the alumni. Accordingly he watches them. Unfortunately, like William Allen White's birds, they also watch him. Inevitably, he has his moments of discouragement when he sees what his institution hath wrought. The professional alumnus can be infinitely disheartening, particularly when he passes his tenth reunion; and as the president delivers his annual greetings to the incoming freshman class, he cannot but view the newest crop of prospective alumni speculatively. Will they too have the recidivistic proclivities of so many of their parents? And yet, hypocrite that he must be if he is to survive, the president warmly welcomes each reunion class with hat (i.e., collection plate) in hand. Such are the occupational hazards of his calling!

Forgive the gentle cynicism, Stanley, for we too are alumni, and when we return to our respective campuses on an occasional June day, let us remember that the president will soon be relaxing in his cabin in the Maine woods. If he looks particularly haggard this year it may stem not so much from months of militancy as from hours of haggling with his board of trustees who, since they are expected to march in the academic procession, always seem to precede the occasion by a plenary meeting. I remember one particularly dreary graduation when the poor man had to preside over the commencement ceremonies despite the fact that the board, a few hours

148

earlier, had relieved him of his presidency, mace and all, effective with the close of the recessional.

College and university governing boards and boards of trustees are, I solemnly believe, essential for the preservation of the public weal; but that makes them no easier to live with. One of my presidential friends always takes the day off after each of his board's monthly meetings. He is utterly exhausted from having to manipulate them around to his liberal way of thinking; and though he is singularly successful, what a price to pay! Student and faculty bodies are usually fairly predictable. Boards of trustees never are. The ideal, perhaps, would be a board that meets only to fire the president and choose his successor. Well, yes, they might in the intervals devote some time and attention to raising funds for the institution. But, unfortunately, they all too often concern themselves not with broad policy matters but rather with administrative details which should rightly be left to the president and his staff.

The latest fad is to have students on the board, a trend which is not without its latent ironies. In one of the English universities I am scheduled to visit in a few days, the faculty recently refused to permit students to serve on the subcommittee of the senate responsibile for faculty promotions, on grounds that they should have no say in personnel matters. However, the board (or in this case the "court") simultaneously voted to accept students as voting members—and the court has final say over all faculty promotions.

Not only is the board's chief responsibility the selection of the president; the president's chief responsibility is the education of his board. A measure of his success is the degree to which he can influence the selection of new members to those boards which are self-perpetuating (rather than politically appointed). A few months ago I had a heart-rending conversation with a young friend who had accepted, rather uncritically, the presidency of a mediocre private university. (It was said of his predecessor that he was a man of no small talent: after all, not every one could have taken a third-rate institution and turned it into a fourth-rate one in only a few short years.) But back to my friend, who approached me in profound discouragement because, having been promised that he could fill the eight vacancies on the board, he had to suffer the experience of seeing the old board reject every one of his candidates. From the little I know of his board he has every reason to feel discouraged. The university will never be any better so long as this particular board is in control.

Some years back I heard the head of a leading faculty organization declare in an address that boards of trustees are vestigial remnants of less sophisticated times and that they are an encumbrance to the successful advancement of a present-day college or university. The way some boards operate I could not but agree. On the other hand, this gentleman's alternative was to turn all control over to the faculty, and although I have considerable faith in participatory democracy, I do not have that much faith!

I have known a few excellent boards, boards that supported, even complemented the president. By and large, though, they are made up of human beings and are subject to all human foibles. There is no question that strict terms of office should be imposed so that no member, however well heeled, can serve longer than eight years or after the age of sixty-five or seventy, whichever is also the mandatory retirement age for the college president. Having a designated number of elected alumni members has rightly gained currency. Even here, if the president works well with the alumni association he can exercise some influence upon whom the alumni select. Too many boards, however, tend to become overbalanced with graduates who serve either as alumni representatives or as regular members. An alumnus, remember, is a man who sees the college as it was and doesn't like to look at what it is.

Having elected student members on the board at best inspires in me a weary "ho-hum." I would certainly not object to seeing it tried, even with the expectation that once aboard the students would never agree to be excluded thereafter. There are, however, other and more effective ways in which the trustees can have the benefits of student perception, and these should be explored if not exhausted before permitting a student to become a voting member of the board just because he happens to be a successful campus politician. Possibly my reservation here is not unrelated to the fact that the president has little or no means of controlling who the student member(s) will be. Or possibly, as I grow older, I become a little more reactionary!

As for faculty membership, I think it can be useful, particularly if the professorial members are drawn from the faculty of some other institution. The president must, it seems to me, be the one and only official representative of the college on the board. Committees of the board can, and often do, meet with faculty representatives, who may well serve even as voting members. But when acting as the agency ultimately responsible for the well-being of the institution neither the board nor the president as *ex officio* member should be obliged to share this final authority with elected representatives of the faculty. Consultation is one thing; sharing authority with individuals who cannot be held accountable and who have an inevitable conflict of interest is quite another. Members of the top administrative staff, even faculty and student observers, may well be encouraged to attend board meetings and even to participate in the discussions; but while their presence can often be helpful, participation must be clearly regulated if the board is to meet its responsibilities and get its business done.

My only direct experience with the presence of a voting faculty representative on a college board of trustees was rather amusing. This individual had fought long and successfully for the principle of representation and was appropriately elected as the first delegate under the new authorization. But in the two years of serving with him I never once heard him open his mouth in a discussion of any significance. I can think of one or two of his faculty colleagues, on the other hand, who would never have closed theirs; so rather than complaining I should perhaps be grateful.

Here at Oxford a month or so ago appeared the Hart Committee report on student participation in governance. In discussing the implications of the report (along with other administrative problems of this rather overawing university), the former vice chancellor, a gentleman and scholar of the old school, said to me, "The students want to run the university; of course we won't let them."

I suppose, Stanley, that my treatment of the movement toward student and faculty participation on the board of trustees has some of the same reactionary flavor.

I promised at the beginning of this letter that it would be the last. Like so many presidential promises this one simply cannot be met. For I really must come back to the question with which we started—whether I can in good conscience advise you to commit yourself to a career in college administration that might lead ultimately to a presidency. Well, let me sleep on it. Tomorrow morning early, before I tackle the problems of that bitterest of tragicomedies by Master Will Shakespeare, I promise to try to sum it all up for your edification.

Good night, sweet prince, flights of angels, and all that. . . .

C. J.

Dear Stanley:

We now come to the aria da capo!

Many long, full, and happy weeks ago you asked my opinion as to whether you should consider a career in academic administration. Little did you think what this innocent query could produce! Obviously, though, I have enjoyed the chance to reflect on its many implications, some of which, I must confess, turned out to be a little remote from the subject. Having once been a dean, I could obviously go on indefinitely; but now that I am dipping my toes tentatively into the half-forgotten waters of Shakespearian scholarship, I would doubtless do well to repeat my master's admonition, "If it were done when 'tis done, then 'twere well it were done quickly." So I'll have at it and bring these musings to a close.

Yes, on average I'd have to say it is a good life. I have enjoyed almost every minute of the hurly-burly, as I believe do most college presidents and deans most of the time. We complain a lot, and when we get together at the wailing wall of our several annual conventions, we may sound like a convocation of morticians. Yet surprisingly few of us leave voluntarily before our appointed hour. Heads fall from time to time and fewer and fewer of my colleagues can boast of long terms of office (no one, even if he survives, should remain longer than ten years), but the woods are full of capable younger men willing to give it a try. And this is as it should be.

At the same time we are a motley crew. I remember walking down the street in Chicago with Marjorie one Saturday afternoon and hearing her say, "Look at that man walking along ahead of us. Doesn't he look like a college president?" She never could explain why she thought so, but he was in fact a college president, the head

153

of a distinguished Eastern university. On the whole, though, there is no such thing as a college-president type, either before or after he is in office. Though we may all share similar psychological aberrations, as nearly as I can tell no two of us are alike. To which I would add, thank Heaven! In the aggregate we may not even be a terribly impressive group. But then, what group is, in the aggregate?

I suspect that among the few characteristics we have in common is a fairly high verbal facility. Our longevity depends on our being able to talk ourselves out of tight corners. We also must be a little thick-skinned, for the office seems ineluctably to attract a certain amount of personal abuse. We have, or develop, the capacity for tolerance; for in our diurnal rounds we encounter an astonishing need for it. The more fortunate among us enjoy low blood pressure—which I have always considered to be my principal natural endowment for the job. Our digestions must be better than average. What luncheon or dinner is complete without a dean or president served up at the high table! And we must be able to sleep at night, some nights—more than most, we have need of what Shakespeare referred to as "nature's soft nurse," sleep.

Rarely can we experience the pleasure that comes so often to the good teacher of knowing that we have constructively influenced someone's life; and yet there is the subtle satisfaction of knowing that we can, at one remove, make it possible for others to bring about change that may affect the future of mankind. In simplest terms, the role of the dean and the president is to provide a climate in which learning can most effectively take place. If this, Stanley, does not sound sufficiently dramatic or even Messianic to meet your inner drives, then stick with "professing." To me it is a humble but exciting mission. To the extent that I may have succeeded in helping others help others to learn, I count this life and this love of college administration well worth the while.

And warmly commend it to you.

Hic jacet,
Charles